D1560482

Amphibians and Reptiles

An Introduction to
Their Natural History and Conservation

Dedication

For Clark, Séamŭs (now known as Fionna),
Cyra and Kiyan, Sierra and Luca, Allison and
James, . . . and all children,

for they

hold the future

of amphibians and reptiles

in their hands.

Amphibians and Reptiles

An Introduction to

Their Natural History and Conservation

by

Marty Crump

The McDonald & Woodward Publishing Company
Granville, Ohio

The McDonald & Woodward Publishing Company
Granville, Ohio
www.mwpubco.com

Amphibians and Reptiles: An Introduction to Their Natural History and Conservation

Text copyright © 2011 by Marty Crump

Printed in Saline, Michigan, by McNaughton & Gunn, Inc.
on paper that meets the minimum requirements of permanence for printed library materials

First printing September 2011

16 15 14 13 12 11   5   4   3   2   1

Library of Congress Cataloging-in-Publication Data

Crump, Martha L.
Amphibians and reptiles : an introduction to their natural history and conservation / by Marty Crump.
   p. cm.
  Rev. ed. of: Amphibians, reptiles, and their conservation. 2002.
  Includes bibliographical references and index.
  ISBN 978-1-935778-20-2 (perfect binding : alk. paper)
   1. Amphibians—Juvenile literature. 2. Reptiles—Juvenile literature. 3. Amphibians—Conservation—Juvenile literature. 4. Reptiles—Conservation—Juvenile literature. I. Crump, Martha L. Amphibians, reptiles, and their conservation. II. Title.
  QL644.2.C78 2011
  597.8—dc23

                                                 2011035499

Contents

Author's Note

This is a revision and update of a book originally published in 2002 by Linnet Press. Much has happened in amphibian and reptile conservation since then. Some major changes and additions in this revision include:

- A new chapter focusing on the key roles that amphibians and reptiles play in aquatic and terrestrial ecosystems.

- A new chapter addressing the parasitic fungus, Bd, that is attacking and killing amphibians on every continent where amphibians occur.

- The addition of new or expanded information, using amphibians and reptiles as examples, that ties in with key science concepts taught in grades 5–8. For example:

  ▶ Structure and function. Gills, lungs, skin, mucous glands, Jacobson's organ, vertebrae, scutes, shell, tail, feet.

  ▶ Reproduction and heredity. Oviparity versus viviparity. Metamorphosis, direct development. Organisms change throughout lifetimes. Species change — evolve — over longer periods of time. Changes related to climate change.

▸ Regulation and behavior. Ectothermy versus endothermy. Migration. Parental care. Food-getting behavior. Herbivory, omnivory, carnivory. Reproductive behavior. Mate attraction and courtship.

▸ Populations and ecosystems. Causes of population declines. Effects of global warming. Food chains and food webs. Interactions of organisms within ecosystems. Change in one species affects many. Effects of non-native species. Role in ecosystem changes with life cycle. Effect of environmental pollution. Threatened and endangered species. Human-caused current extinction.

▸ Diversity and adaptations of organisms. Diversity of amphibians and reptiles. Classification. Geographic distribution. Life cycles. Adaptations to terrestrial, arboreal, fossorial, aquatic living. Survival in environment (protective coloration and other anti-predator defenses).

● Updated 2010 figures on the IUCN Red List of Threatened Species; updated 2011 figures on human population growth, the United States Endangered Species Act, and CITES protected species.

● Addition of color plates and many more black and white images in text; two tables; two pie diagrams.

Acknowledgments

While writing a chapter on the conservation of amphibians and reptiles for the college textbook *Herpetology*, I thought, "Why not share this information with kids?" After all, they are the generation that will have a major impact on the future of amphibians and reptiles. They will be the voters of tomorrow. They will set the policies of tomorrow. And they will raise the children of tomorrow. Thus, I'm grateful to Harvey Pough for inviting me to be a co-author of the *Herpetology* textbook.

Many people read the manuscript for this book and offered valuable suggestions. For their help I thank Annie Crego and her students Michael Blancarte (5th grade) and Natasha Slaughter (6th grade); Darcie Whitney and her students Ben Bennett and Peter Bremer (7th graders) and Jennifer Dunn and Holland Wilberger (8th graders); Peter Feinsinger; Karen Hackler; Judy Hendrickson; and Jenny Vollman.

Many thanks go to friends and colleagues who provided photographs for this revised and updated edition: Brady Barr, Dick Bartlett, Judith Bryja and the Houston Zoo, Danté Fenolio, Karen Hackler, Bob Henderson, Joe Mitchell, Bekky Muscher, and Rich Sajdak. Helena Guindon generously allowed me to include her cartoons, and Frank Hensley made the pie diagrams.

I thank Jerry McDonald of McDonald & Woodward Publishing Company for believing in this book and for his guidance and support.

Amphibians and Reptiles

1

Too Weird to Be True?

They come in every color of the rainbow and more: rose, lemon yellow, tangerine, lavender, sky blue, jungle green, chocolate, ebony, and ivory. They eat just about everything, from algae and bacteria to water buffalo. They range in length from smaller than 1 inch to more than 25 feet. They live on land, underground, in trees, in the ocean, and in ponds, lakes, and rivers. They walk, run, hop, crawl, climb, slither, glide, and swim. What are they? They're amphibians and reptiles. And they are awesome!

Appearance

Some amphibians and reptiles are brightly colored (Plates 1–4). The Brazilian horned frog is green, yellow, orange, brown, and cream. One harlequin frog is pink and black. Several kinds of salamanders are blood red with black spots. Various chameleons are spotted yellow-orange, vermilion, violet, turquoise, or emerald green. Some male chameleons become much brighter when they court females or confront other males. Painted turtles look as though someone painted their shells with stripes and splotches of green, yellow, orange, and black. In sunlight, the scales of rainbow boas give off iridescent hues of green, blue, and purple.

Some amphibians and reptiles have amazing bodies that seem too weird to be true (Plates 5–8). Horned treefrogs, with their bizarre-shaped triangular heads, look like creatures from another planet. Surinam toads resemble burnt, 4-legged pancakes. Amphiuma salamanders paddle through the water on four ridiculously tiny legs. Mexican mole lizards, pink in color, tunnel underground with their clawed front legs — their only legs (Figure 1). Matamata turtles snorkel above the surface of rivers with their long, fleshy Pinocchio-like snouts. Flying dragon lizards glide through the air by spreading out flaps of skin along the sides of their bodies. Vine snakes can balance their 2-foot-long, skinny bodies on your finger.

Figure 1. Mexican mole lizards have two front legs, one of which can be seen at right, but no back legs. These lizards live in deserts and dry scrub lands where they use their front feet to burrow underground.

2

Defense

Because most amphibians and reptiles have many different types of predators, they have more than one defense to protect themselves. Many rely on *camouflage** — blending in with the surroundings — as a first line of defense. If that doesn't work, spitting cobras spit venom and aim for their attackers' eyes. Toads urinate and garter snakes defecate when grabbed by predators. Horned lizards squirt blood from the corners of their eyes. Some salamanders and gecko lizards spray or ooze sticky secretions from their tails onto predators. While the predator tries to disentangle itself, the salamander or gecko escapes.

Toxic chemicals of some amphibians and reptiles can sicken or kill predators. *Poisonous* animals, for example some frogs and salamanders, secrete toxins from skin glands. If a predator tries to eat the amphibian, it gets a mouthful of poison. Most poisonous amphibians won't hurt you unless you rub your eyes after handling them, or unless the toxin gets into a cut. *Venomous* snakes, for example coral snakes and rattlesnakes, have toxin glands in their mouths. Teeth or fangs connected to these glands inject the toxin into another animal.

Many poisonous and venomous animals are brightly colored. These colors warn would-be predators of the animals' toxicity. Poison dart frogs, in shades of blue, purple, green, orange, yellow, and red, warn: "Don't eat me. I'm poisonous." Fire salamanders convey the same message in vivid yellow and black. Coral snakes warn with red, yellow, and black rings.

---

* Italicized words are defined in the glossary.

Figure 2. When disturbed, a hognose snake hisses loudly. If the predator approaches, the snake strikes. If that doesn't deter the attacker, the snake writhes about, urinates, and defecates. Finally, it flips onto its back, opens its mouth, and pretends to be dead.

Cobras spread their hoods in a threat display, and rattlesnakes shake their rattles to warn would-be predators. When attacked, hognose snakes roll over and play dead — usually with their tongues hanging out of their open mouths (Figure 2). Some treefrogs roll onto their backs and play dead (Figure 3). Most predators don't eat dead animals, so they drop their seemingly dead catch. Many kinds of salamanders and lizards purposely let part of their tails break off when predators grab them. The predator focuses its attention on the wiggling tail, and the salamander or lizard escapes.

If nothing else works, some amphibians and reptiles fight back by biting, clawing, or smacking their tails against their attackers.

Figure 3. When I picked up this leaf frog, it rolled over, curled up, and played dead. Now it doesn't look like something to eat.

Care for Their Young

Although most amphibians abandon their eggs, some are terrific parents. Mother marsupial treefrogs carry their fertilized eggs in pouches on their backs. Some mother and father frogs stand guard to protect their eggs from spiders and other predators (Figure 4). Frog parents can be feisty. Father gladiator frogs defend their eggs from other males by wrestling and digging sharp thumb spines into their opponents' eyes and ears. Some frog parents hiss and lunge at predators that try to

Figure 4. This father mountain coqui from Puerto Rico is guarding his eggs from predators.

Figure 5. Male Darwin's frogs brood tadpoles in their vocal sacs. While brooding, they can eat but they cannot call.

eat their eggs. Male Japanese giant salamanders rock back and forth near their eggs in the water, which increases the flow of oxygen over them. Female marbled salamanders roll their terrestrial eggs, which kills fungal growth. Female mountain dusky salamanders also move their eggs around, and they eat any of their eggs that die. By doing so, they prevent growth of fungi that might attack their surviving eggs.

Male Darwin's frogs from Chile and Argentina watch over their 3 to 8 fertilized eggs for about 20 days. When the eggs are about ready to hatch, the father slurps them into his mouth. From there the eggs slip down into his *vocal sac*, the balloon-like pouch in the throat area that fills with air when a male frog calls (Figure 5). The eggs soon hatch into tadpoles. The father carries his tadpoles in his vocal sac until the babies *metamorphose* (transform, or change) into little frogs about 50 days later. Then, he opens his mouth, and the little frogs hop out.

Some reptiles care for their young. Mother alligators and crocodiles usually stay near their nests after they lay their eggs. They chase and bite intruders. When the young hatch, the mothers rip open their nests and carry their babies in their mouths to water. The females stay near their young, sometimes for a year or more, and protect them from predators. Some fathers help defend their eggs and, later, their young ones.

Some snakes are also caring parents. Females of several kinds of pythons coil around their eggs (Figure 6). By twitching their bodies they contract their muscles and generate heat, which warms the eggs. Female African forest cobras lay their eggs in nests of leaves. As the vegetation decays, heat is

Figure 6. A female pygmy python, the smallest python in the world, broods her eggs. These 20 to 24 inch pythons live in western Australia.

generated, which helps to keep the eggs warm. Both the mother and father guard the nest.

Food and Food-getting Behavior

Adult amphibians eat other animals, especially insects. Although some lizards and turtles eat mushrooms, flowers, leaves, berries and other fruit, or seaweed, most reptiles eat other animals. Amphibians and reptiles with large mouths feast on large prey — fishes, other amphibians and reptiles, birds, and mammals. Narrow-mouth toads and horned lizards eat mainly ants and termites. Goo-eater snakes prefer slugs and snails.

African egg-eating snakes swallow bird eggs that are three times the width of their heads. That's equivalent to you swallowing a large watermelon — whole! The snake crushes the shell in its throat, swallows the inside of the egg, and vomits the shell.

Many amphibians and reptiles actively search for prey among fallen leaves on the ground, on tree trunks and leaves high in the canopy, or anywhere in between. Others lie in wait for insects or other moving prey. Then they pounce. Some congregate around lights at night and eat moths, beetles, and other insects attracted to the light.

Komodo dragons, which can grow to be 10 feet long and weigh more than 200 pounds, ambush small deer, wild boar, and even water buffalo. The lizards have deadly bacteria in their saliva. When the lizards bite into prey, the bacteria infect the wound and eventually kill the animal. Komodo dragons can sniff out dead animals from 7 miles away. Many Komodo dragons gather at a rotting carcass and feast. They also eat dead animals not killed by themselves (Figure 7).

Horned frogs, often called "pac-man frogs," have mouths so big they look like hopping mouths with legs attached (Plate 1). They eat other frogs, lizards, baby birds, and mice. A pac-man frog sometimes twitches its long, skinny toe to mimic a moving insect. When a frog hops over to check out the possible meal, the owner of the toe eats the frog instead.

Some reptiles also catch their dinners by trickery (Figure 8). A Saharan sand viper lies buried in the sand. Only its eyes and snout peek above the surface. If the snake detects a lizard nearby, it pokes its black-and-white banded tail above the sand and slowly wiggles it. When the lizard lunges at what seems to

Figure 7. Komodo dragons, the largest lizards in the world, get their food in three major ways. They ambush active prey, attack sleeping animals, and eat dead animals such as these fish washed up onto the beach.

Figure 8. An alligator snapping turtle opens its mouth and wiggles a pink worm-like flap of skin on its tongue. When a fish swims into the mouth to eat the worm, the turtle eats the fish.

be food, the snake strikes, injects venom into the lizard, and eats it. Young copperheads have yellow tails (Plate 3). They lure frogs by wiggling their tail tips. As copperheads grow, they switch to eating rodents. Their tails change color to blend in with the rest of their bodies. The snakes stop the luring behavior as well.

Interesting as these isolated tidbits of information are, they really don't tell us much about reptiles and amphibians. For that, we need to dig deeper. We need to look at not only the unusual and bizarre animals, but the "everyday" ones as well.

2

What Are
Amphibians and Reptiles?

*H*erpetology is the study of amphibians and reptiles. The word comes from the Greek words *herpeton,* meaning "crawling thing," and *logos*, meaning "knowledge." Why are wet-to-the-touch salamanders and frogs lumped together with armored alligators and scaly snakes? The reason is that 200 years ago, people considered the differences between amphibians and reptiles to be relatively minor. They called all of these animals amphibians. Amphibians and reptiles are similar in some ways but now we know that they also are very different in many ways. Even though amphibians and reptiles are different in many ways, they are still grouped together by scientists. They're often called "herpetofauna," "herps," or "herptiles." Scientists who study amphibians and reptiles are called *herpetologists*.

How Are Amphibians and Reptiles
Similar to Each Other?

All amphibians and reptiles have a skeleton that includes a spinal column, or backbone, that helps support the body. The backbone is made up of bones called vertebrae. Humans also have vertebrae made of bone, as do all other mammals, birds, and bony fishes. The subphylum Vertebrata is divided into seven groups, called *classes*. Humans belong to the class Mammalia, amphibians belong to the class Amphibia, and reptiles belong to the class Reptilia, as illustrated in the sidebar "Scientific Classification."

Backbones aren't the only feature that amphibians and reptiles share. Both groups are *ectothermic*. In order to raise their body temperatures high enough to be active, they need an outside source of heat to warm their bodies. This external source of heat is the sun. To acquire this heat, these animals either bask in the sun or rest on a warm surface, such as a rock or mud warmed by the sun.

Amphibians and reptiles are often said to be "cold-blooded." Ectothermic is the correct term, however, because on a warm day their blood isn't cold. Instead, their body temperature stays about the same as their surroundings. In the early morning a lizard is sluggish. It is cold (and its blood is cold) because the ground it sits on is cold. After the lizard basks in the sun for awhile, its body temperature warms up (Figure 9). The lizard scampers off and hunts for food. Later in the day, it may move into shade because its body is too hot. Shuttling back and forth between sun and shade, and by seeking shelter, the lizard keeps its body at a good temperature.

Mammals and birds are *endothermic*. These animals have built-in control of their body temperature. Endotherms produce heat chemically, inside their bodies, by breaking down food. In this way they maintain a constant high body temperature even when the temperature of the environment constantly changes. Because it takes a lot of energy to do this, birds and mammals need to eat a lot more food than do amphibians and reptiles. At least 90% of the energy a human gets from food goes into maintaining its body temperature. The same goes for other endotherms. This means that less than 10% of the energy in food is left for growth or reproduction. In contrast, between 30 and 90% of the energy an amphibian or reptile gets from its food is used for growth or reproduction. Ectotherms and endotherms represent two very different ways of living.

Scientific Classification

Humans everywhere recognize and name different kinds of animals, plants, and other living organisms. The Jivaro Indians of eastern Ecuador have individual names for each plant they consider edible, poisonous, or medicinal. Likewise, the Masai people of Kenya, the Pygmies of the Congo River Basin, and the Bushmen of the Kalahari Desert have names for each plant and animal important to them — each in their own language.

Long ago, naturalists and scientists realized they needed a standard system of grouping and naming organisms so they could communicate with each other worldwide. They developed a system of scientific classification. Organisms within a group are more similar to each other than they are to organisms that belong to other groups. Scientific names are derived from either Latin or Greek words, because the early scholars who classified organisms used these languages.

Carolus Linnaeus, a Swedish naturalist, developed the scientific classification system we use today. It has lasted since 1753. There are seven main levels in the Linnean hierarchy, though many are further broken down into subgroups. From highest to lowest, these are: kingdom, phylum, class, order, family, genus, and species.

We currently recognize six kingdoms. All animals belong to the kingdom Animalia. The other five kingdoms include such organisms as plants, fungi, bacteria, and algae. Each kingdom is made up of subdivisions, or groups, called phyla (phylum, singular). Animalia consists of 36 phyla. One of these is Chordata. All animals that have a notochord (a rod-like cord that runs down the body and provides support) during some stage of their lives are grouped in the phylum Chordata. A major subgroup, or subphylum, of Chordata is Vertebrata. Most, but not all, vertebrates have backbones made up of vertebrae. The more than 50,000 living species of vertebrates are divided into seven classes: Agnatha (jawless fishes, such as lamprey), Chondrichthyes (cartilaginous fishes, such as sharks), Osteichthyes (bony fishes, such as trout), Amphibia (amphibians, such as bullfrogs), Reptilia (reptiles, such as garter snakes), Aves (birds, such as robins), and Mammalia (mammals, such as dogs).

Each class is divided into orders. Consider the reptiles. The class Reptilia consists of 4 orders: Testudines (turtles), Crocodylia (crocodilians), Squamata (lizards and snakes), and Rhynchocephalia (tuatara). The fifth level is family. The order Testudines consists of 13 families of turtles alive today. One is Testudinidae, to which box turtles, African pancake tortoises, and Galápagos tortoises belong.

The sixth level is genus. Like all levels above it, the name of a genus is always capitalized. Unlike the names of those higher levels, however, the genus name is always italicized or underlined. Galápagos tortoises and gopher tortoises are both in the genus *Geochelone*. The seventh level is that of species, but — unlike the higher-level groups just named — the name of every species is made up of two words that form what is called a binomium. The first of these two words is the name of the genus in which the species occurs. The second is the specific epithet. The specific epithet is never capitalized but, like the genus, it is always italicized or underlined. The specific epithet of the Galápagos tortoise is *gigantea*; the specific epithet of the gopher tortoise is *polyphemus.* When the genus and specific epithet are combined to provide the taxonomic names of these two species of tortoises, we get *Geochelone gigantea* for the Galápagos tortoise and *Geochelone polyphemus* for the gopher tortoise.

Four Examples of Scientific Classification

Taxonomic Level	Humans	Red-Legged Frog
1. Kingdom	Animalia	Animalia
2. Phylum	Chordata	Chordata
3. Class	Mammalia	Amphibia
4. Order	Primates	Anura
5. Family	Hominidae	Ranidae
6. Genus	*Homo*	*Rana*
Specific epithet*	*sapiens*	*aurora*
7. Species	*Homo sapiens*	*Rana aurora*

Taxonomic Level	Komodo Dragon	Snapping Turtle
1. Kingdom	Animalia	Animalia
2. Phylum	Chordata	Chordata
3. Class	Reptilia	Reptilia
4. Order	Squamata	Testudines
5. Family	Varanidae	Chelydridae
6. Genus	*Varanus*	*Chelydra*
Specific epithet*	*komodoensis*	*serpentina*
7. Species	*Varanus komodoensis*	*Chelydra serpentina*

* The "specific epithet" is not a taxonomic level; rather, it is a word that follows the name of a genus to make up a binomium, the two-word combination that is the name of a species.

Figure 9. Male marine iguanas, from the Galápagos Islands, stay on their territories to protect them from intruding males. In the morning when the lizards are cold, they orient their bodies perpendicular to the sun's rays to absorb the maximum amount of heat. When they get too hot by midday, they face the sun and lift the front part of their bodies off the ground. That way they minimize the amount of heat they absorb.

How Are Amphibians and Reptiles Different from Each Other?

The most obvious difference between amphibians and reptiles is their skin (Figure 10). Reptiles have dry skin and scales that help keep their bodies from losing moisture. Some live in deserts and other dry places. Their scales are made of *keratin*, a protein also found in human fingernails and bird feathers. Instead of scales, an amphibian's skin is covered with mucus

Figure 10. Top: Amphibians, such as this cave salamander, have mucous glands scattered over their skin. These glands help to keep the skin moist. **Bottom:** Reptiles, such as this dwarf iguana, have dry skin and scales.

produced by glands. Without mucus, an amphibian on dry land would die. Amphibians do part of their breathing through their skin, but this only works if the skin is moist.

Amphibians and reptiles reproduce in different ways. Most amphibians, even many that live out of water as adults, lay their eggs in water and the eggs hatch into larvae. Amphibian eggs have jelly capsules surrounding and protecting the embryos (Figure 11). Amphibian eggs dry out easily, so they must develop either in water or in very moist environments out of water. The eggs of most frogs and toads hatch into larvae, called tadpoles. In both salamanders and caecilians (long, thin amphibians without legs), the young are just called larvae.

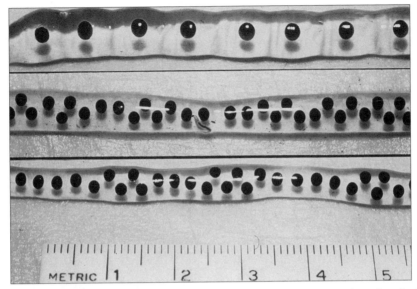

Figure 11. Amphibian eggs are surrounded by jelly capsules that help to keep the embryos moist. Toad eggs are deposited as strings; the capsule of one egg is connected to the capsule of the egg on each side of it.

Figure 12. These Suwannee cooter (turtle) eggs have been dug out from their nest. Reptile eggs are protected by shells.

All reptiles that lay eggs, even the ones that spend most of their lives in water, lay their eggs on land (Figure 12). Why don't the eggs dry out? One reason is that inside the egg, a reptile embryo floats in its own fluid, surrounded by a membrane called the *amnion*. Another reason is that the outside of a reptile egg is covered with a shell that protects the embryo. Some reptile eggs have brittle shells, like birds' eggs; others have tough leathery shells. Tiny pores in the shell allow the embryo to breathe. Oxygen passes into the embryo and carbon dioxide passes out.

Not all amphibians and reptiles lay eggs. In some kinds of frogs, salamanders, caecilians, lizards, and snakes, the young develop inside the mother's body, and she gives birth to fully formed young just as most mammals do.

Each animal species has a *life cycle*, or stages that it passes through from birth until death. Reptiles and some amphibians hatch from their eggs as miniature adults or are born from

Figure 13. Notice the feathery, external gills of this flatwood salamander larva.

20

their mothers as miniature adults. These young grow, in time become reproductively mature, and eventually die.

In contrast, most amphibians have *complex life cycles.* The female lays her eggs, usually in water, and the eggs hatch as larvae. The larval body form is very different from the adult body form (Figure 13). *Metamorphosis* is the process of change from the larval body form to the adult form. Amphibians that have complex life cycles generally spend the larval stage in water. After they metamorphose, the juveniles and adults either live on land or they shuttle back and forth between land and water.

Read on to find out more about the fascinating lives of amphibians.

3 Meet the Amphibians

The word amphibian comes from the Greek words *amphi*, meaning double, and *bios*, meaning life. This is an appropriate name, because many amphibians live in the water and on land at different times of their lives. Most begin as eggs in water and end up as adults on land, but there are exceptions. Some amphibians are completely *aquatic* (live in the water), and others are entirely *terrestrial* (live on land), throughout their lives.

Scientists divide the class Amphibia into three groups, or *orders* (Figure 14). The largest order is Anura — the frogs. Anura comes from the Greek words *an* and *oura* meaning "without tail." Adult frogs don't have tails. Salamanders belong to the order Urodela, from the Greek words *uro* and *delos* meaning "tail evident." All salamanders have tails — some short and fat, others long and skinny. The third order, unfamiliar to most people, is the Gymnophiona, the caecilians. Caecilians are long, thin amphibians without legs. Gymnophiona comes from the Greek words *gymnos* and *ophis* meaning "naked serpent." Caecilians look like snakes without scales.

Order Anura: Frogs

There are many more *species* of frogs than members of the other two orders of amphibians combined (Figure 15). New

Figure 14. The class Amphibia is composed of three orders: **Top left:** Anura (frogs, such as this gladiator frog), **Top right:** Urodela (salamanders, such as this three-lined salamander), and **Bottom:** Gymnophiona (caecilians, such as this West African caecilian).

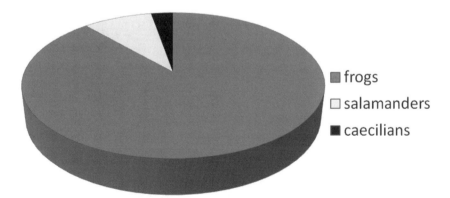

Figure 15. Of the approximately 6714 species of amphibians, the frogs (Anura) represent by far the largest order with about 5940 species.

species are discovered every year, especially in tropical areas where there are still many unexplored places. Scientists currently recognize about 5940 species of frogs. Although most species are *nocturnal* (active at night), some are *diurnal* (active during the day).

Adult frogs have four legs, and they lack tails. Most have strong hind legs, well-suited for jumping. Body shapes range from pointed snouts connected to thin, long torsos to snub noses connected to ping-pong ball figures. There may be webs between the fingers and toes, or not. Some frogs are covered with warty bumps filled with poison. Others have smooth skin. Some have bony horns on their heads (Plate 5). Others have flaps of skin on their noses, eyelids, or legs.

Fossorial (burrowing) frogs generally have short hind legs. Some have small heads with pointed snouts. Spadefoot toads have spade-like structures on their hind feet used for digging. Aquatic frogs generally have long hind legs and fully webbed feet (Figure 16). Many aquatic frogs have eyes on the tops of their heads rather than at the sides. *Arboreal* (living in the trees) frogs often have long hind legs and expanded toe pads. The pads help grip leaves and stems.

What's the difference between frogs and toads? All toads are frogs but not all frogs are toads (Figure 17). Think about dogs. All poodles are dogs but not all dogs are poodles. Toads are one type of frog, and poodles are one type of dog. The word toad is usually used for frogs that have drier skin, squat and warty bodies, and hind legs that aren't very powerful. Toads tend to "flop" when they jump, in contrast to the Olympic-style

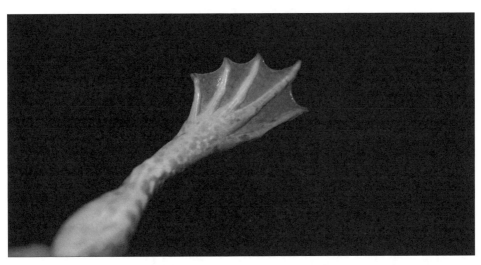

Figure 16. The full web on the hind foot of this bullfrog allows the frog to swim efficiently. That's also why human divers wear rubber flippers on their feet.

Figure 17. Top: Rococo toads from Argentina have 8-inch-long fat, squat, and warty bodies. **Bottom:** Amazon river frogs live in northern South America. They reach 5 inches in length and have smooth skin and long legs. They are related to bullfrogs and leopard frogs in the United States.

25

leaps that many other frogs make. Another difference is that most toads don't have teeth, whereas most other frogs do. Since all toads are frogs, when you read the word frog here, think toad too!

Frogs live just about everywhere except in some extremely dry deserts, on some islands, and near the North and South poles. More species live in wet tropical environments than anywhere else. For example, the country of Ecuador in South America and the state of Colorado are about the same size. Ecuador has about 434 species of frogs. Colorado has 17. The state of Florida is about three times larger than the country of Costa Rica, in Central America. Costa Rica has 133 species of frogs, but Florida has only 33.

Males of most frogs call to attract females during the mating season (Plate 9). Each species has its own particular call. Females recognize and respond only to the calls given by males of their own species. Calls are more than just "ribbets" and "croaks." They include grunts, peeps, trills, bonks, squawks, tinks, whistles, and clicks. Calls may be single notes, or groups of repeated notes. Some are melodious. Others are downright irritating to the human ear. Large frogs have deep voices. Smaller species have higher calls. In a few species, females also have a voice, but their call is much softer than the male's call. These females use their voice to communicate to males just before mating.

Sound waves go through the frog's external ear and into the inner ear. The external ear, a thin membrane of skin, is called the tympanum. In most frogs, the tympanum is about

Figure 18. Is this adult green frog a male or a female? How do you know?

the same size in males and females, or a little larger in females. In some frogs of the family Ranidae, however, the tympanum is much larger in males. In female bullfrogs and green frogs, for example, the tympanum is about the same size as the eye or a little smaller. In male bullfrogs and green frogs, the tympanum is much larger than the eye (Figure 18). What do these differences mean? We don't know, but since the tympanum is visible in a living frog, it's a handy way for people to tell the sexes apart!

Once a male frog has attracted a female and she is ready to mate, he climbs onto her back and clasps her with his legs (Figure 19). This position is called *amplexus*. As she releases her eggs, he fertilizes them externally. A few species have internal fertilization, but the vast majority of frogs fertilize the eggs externally.

Figure 19. These dink frogs are in amplexus — the mating position. The larger frog underneath is the female; the smaller one on top is the male.

Most frogs are *oviparous* — they lay eggs. Generally they lay their eggs in water, and the eggs hatch into tadpoles. Toads lay their eggs in strings, like beads on a necklace (Figure 11). Some frogs lay their eggs in clumps. Others scatter them individually around the pond. Newly hatched tadpoles breathe through gills. Tadpoles that live in warm ponds, where there isn't much oxygen, soon begin to develop lungs. These tadpoles swim to the surface and gulp air. In contrast, water in cool mountain streams has plenty of oxygen. Tadpoles that live there don't develop their lungs until shortly before they *metamorphose* into froglets.

Unless hiding from predators or sleeping, most tadpoles eat constantly. Most are *herbivorous* (feeding on plants), and they eat a lot of algae. Some are *carnivorous* (eating animals). These eat insects, worms, and even other tadpoles, including their own species. Others are *omnivorous* — they eat both plants and animals.

A tadpole doesn't suddenly wake up and find itself transformed into a frog. As it grows, a tadpole's body changes in many ways. The long, coiled intestine ideal for digesting algae and plant material shortens into an adult-type gut ideal for digesting animal matter. Moveable eyelids form. Skin glands mature. Legs develop — first the hind legs, then the front ones (Figure 20). Mouth parts change and a tongue develops. The bones harden. The tail shrinks to nothing, and the tadpole is now a frog. What started off as an algae-eating, swimming blob attached to a tail, ends up as a big-mouthed predator hopping or flopping about on four sturdy legs.

Instead of laying their eggs in the water, some frogs lay them inside fallen logs, in clumps of wet moss, in cavities, or in other moist sites where the eggs won't dry out. In some of these species, the eggs hatch into tadpoles that stay in their moist nests and develop without ever going into the water. They

Figure 20. This green tree frog tadpole has well-developed hind legs. Its left front leg is about ready to break through the skin. It won't be long before it has four legs and its tail begins to shrink.

Figure 21. Bokermann's treefrog lays its eggs on leaves overhanging the water. After developing for a few more days, these tadpoles will break through their jelly capsules and flip into the water below.

hatch with huge bellyfuls of yolk, and they grow by absorbing the yolk. They don't eat until after they metamorphose.

In certain other species, tadpoles that hatch away from water must get to water or they'll die. Glass frogs, leaf frogs, and some other frogs lay their eggs on leaves hanging above water (Figure 21). As they hatch, the tadpoles flip out of their jelly capsules and somersault into the water below. Female marsupial frogs carry their eggs in pouches on their backs. In some of these species, after the tadpoles hatch the mother dips into a puddle or pond. Using her hind feet, she pushes the tadpoles out of her pouch and into the water. Poison frogs lay their eggs on land. Depending on the species, either the mother or father watches over the eggs until they hatch. The tadpoles wriggle up onto the parent and ride piggyback until the parent shrugs them off into water (Figure 22).

Figure 22. Male spot-legged poison frogs transport their tadpoles to water.

Some terrestrial eggs take a long time to develop, never pass through a tadpole stage, and hatch as miniature frogs (Figure 23). This is called *direct development*. Most frogs with direct development live in wet tropical rain forests or cloud forests. In some species the mother or father stays with the eggs and urinates on them to keep them moist. The parent might also protect the eggs from predators. If the predator is a small insect or spider, the parent might simply eat it. If the intruder is another frog trying to eat the eggs, the parent might bite the intruder's head, block it from getting to the eggs, or wrestle to defend its young.

Two of my favorite frogs from South America (Plate 5) have direct development, but they go about this in bizarre and very

Figure 23. These Costa Rican dink frog eggs were deposited between moist leaves on the ground. The eggs will undergo direct development. When they hatch, miniature dink frogs will pop out — not tadpoles.

different ways. Aquatic female Surinam toads carry their eggs embedded in the skin on their backs. When time to hatch, miniature frogs emerge from their mother's skin and swim away. Terrestrial female egg-brooding horned treefrogs carry up to 30 eggs on their backs. Mucous glands from the mother's skin secrete a sticky substance that keeps the eggs in place. If this species is similar to its close relatives, each hatchling frog is attached to its mother by a pair of cords — "gill stalks" still connected to the egg capsule. Soon the cords will break and free the babies from their mother's back.

Five species of frogs don't lay eggs at all. Instead, they're *viviparous.* The young develop inside the mother and are born as miniature frogs. In three of these, the young absorb their yolk while developing. In the other two, the young feed on substances secreted from inside the mother's oviduct — the part of the mother's body where the young develop.

Adult frogs breathe through lungs and through their skin. The skin is so thin that oxygen can pass through and enter tiny blood vessels called capillaries. Red blood cells then carry the oxygen throughout the body. This system of breathing doesn't work well if the skin gets too dry. As long as a frog is in a moist environment, its skin glands produce enough mucus to keep the skin in good working order for breathing.

The aquatic Lake Titicaca frog, which lives in Lake Titicaca on the border between Peru and Bolivia, does much of its breathing through its skin (Plate 10). At the frogs' elevation of about 12,500 feet above sea level, both air and water are low in oxygen concentration. These frogs have large, baggy folds of skin along the sides of their bodies, which increases skin surface area and allows for extra absorption of oxygen. The frogs slowly sway back and forth in the water. This activity helps to allow water with oxygen to contact the skin and for water with carbon dioxide to be carried away from the frog.

The diets of adult frogs are nearly as varied as the animals themselves. Almost all are carnivorous. Most eat any kind of insect, earthworm, or other *invertebrate* as long as it's the right size. Some species, however, eat only certain types of food, such as ants and termites. Ant- and termite-eating frogs often have small heads and narrow mouths that don't open very widely (Figure 24). In contrast, frogs with large heads and wide mouths can grab hold of and eat large insects, other frogs, snakes, lizards, and even small birds and mammals (Figure 24).

Figure 24. Top: This African shovelnose frog has a small, narrow mouth — perfectly suited for eating ants and termites. **Bottom:** The large, wide mouth of this African bullfrog allows it to eat other frogs, reptiles, birds, and rodents.

Most frogs capture their prey by flicking out their sticky tongues, slapping them onto the victims, and then flipping the tongues back into their mouths with lightning speed. The only known herbivorous frog eats fruit.

Frogs protect themselves in many ways. Often the first line of defense is simply to avoid being seen. Many species are cryptic or *camouflaged*. They blend in with their background, such as when a brown toad squats on mud or a green treefrog perches on a leaf. Once a predator spies a frog, the frog might jump to escape. If the predator catches up, the frog might launch into another defense. Some frogs flip over and play dead (Plate 11). American toads crouch and become immobile (Plate 11). Some bloat themselves by filling their lungs with air. Now the frog seems too big to eat.

Leaf frogs trick predators by suddenly looking different. A green frog on a green leaf is hard for a predator to see. But the frog can't sit on the leaf forever. When it walks or hops, a green leaf frog exposes contrasting colors of stripes or spots on its flanks (Plate 1). This is called flash coloration. A predator seeing the moving frog presumably cues in on this contrasting pattern. Even a color-blind predator would see the pattern. When the frog lands, it pulls its legs close to its body and the contrasting pattern disappears. The frog no longer looks like what the predator perceived as food.

Some frogs have poisonous skin. Many of these frogs, such as harlequin frogs and poison dart frogs, are brightly colored. Their colors warn potential predators that they are poisonous (Plate 12). Other frogs with toxin, such as toads, are camouflaged. Some toads have large *parotoid* glands behind their eyes (Figure 25). If a predator grabs one of these toads, white poisonous mucus oozes out from the glands. In some toads, the fluid merely tastes foul or burns. In others, such as the Colorado river toad, the mucus causes muscle spasms, irregular heartbeat, and breathing problems for the attacker.

Frogs range from tiny creatures half an inch long to the goliath frog from west-Central Africa, a giant that can reach 12 inches. Most species are somewhere in between these extremes, with body lengths of 1 to 6 inches.

Figure 25. Colorado river toads have large parotoid glands, identified here by arrows, behind their eyes. If a predator gets parotoid secretion from one of these toads in its mouth, it will feel mighty uncomfortable!

Order Urodela: Salamanders

The second largest order of amphibians is Urodela — the salamanders (Figure 26). At first glance salamanders resemble lizards, but if you look closely you won't see scales. Instead, salamanders have moist skin, thanks to their mucous glands. Also, lizards have claws on their toes; salamanders don't. Almost all salamanders have four legs, though sirens have only two (Plate 7).

There are about 588 species of salamanders alive today. Most live in Europe, Asia, and North America. Some live in Central and South America. There are none in Australia and only a few in extreme northern Africa.

Most salamanders live on the ground or in the water, but some climb trees and others burrow underground. Some aquatic salamanders are long and thin. Others have flattened,

Figure 26. Salamanders, such as this California tiger salamander, belong to the order Urodela.

robust bodies. Most arboreal salamanders are small. They have webbed feet, and some have prehensile tails that wrap around and grasp stems and twigs. Prehensile tails are a great adaptation for moving around in vegetation. Salamanders that burrow under the ground generally have small but long slender bodies and small legs and feet.

Some cave salamanders have white skin, and their eyes are tiny and useless (Figure 27; Plate 7). They're skinny, and their legs are spindly. Overall, they don't look very healthy. But they are. They're just adapted to a unique environment where there's no light.

Like frogs, salamanders breathe in several ways. Fully aquatic species generally breathe through gills, but some also poke their snouts out of the water and breathe through their lungs. The lungs of aquatic salamanders serve a second

Figure 27. The pinkish-white grotto salamander lives in caves. Although the larvae have functional eyes, the adults are blind.

function: they help the animals to stay at a certain depth. When there's a lot of air in its lungs, the salamander will float. To eat invertebrates from the bottom mud, the salamander exhales some air from its lungs and sinks. Aquatic salamanders also breathe through their skin. Fully aquatic hellbenders live in mountain streams in the eastern United States (Plate 7). Like Lake Titicaca frogs, hellbenders have folds of skin along the sides of their bodies. They also sway back and forth in the water, which increases oxygen absorption. Most terrestrial salamanders breathe both through lungs and skin. One large family of salamanders, the Plethodontidae, lacks lungs (Figure 28). These "lungless salamanders" breathe through their skin and the moist lining of their mouths.

Salamanders don't peep and squawk to communicate with each other. And they're rather near-sighted. They can't see another salamander unless it's close by. At close range, they communicate with each other by raising or flattening their bodies or by waving their tails. Salamanders also communicate by touch and smell.

Courtship among salamanders often involves physical contact (Figure 29). For example, the male may rub his chin glands against the female. These glands contain chemicals called pheromones that encourage the female to mate. Males of some species are more aggressive. They slap their chins against the females. Some even bite or scratch the females with their teeth and then rub their glands on the open areas.

Figure 28. Nauta mushroom-tongue salamanders, a species of lungless salamander, live in Colombia, Venezuela, Ecuador, Peru, Bolivia, and Brazil. They live in moist environments and breathe only from their skin and the lining of their mouths.

Figure 29. A male red-spotted newt grabs a female and wraps his back legs around her neck. He rubs her snout with glands on the side of his head. These glands contain chemicals called pheromones that stimulate the female to mate.

By doing this, the pheromones quickly enter the females' bloodstreams.

Salamanders reproduce in various ways. Some lay eggs in the water, and the eggs hatch into aquatic larvae that eventually metamorphose into the adult body form. Other species lay eggs on land. After a period of direct development, a miniature version of an adult salamander hatches. In many direct-developing salamanders, the mother protects the eggs from drying out and defends them against predators. Four species of salamanders are viviparous. In two of these, the young absorb their yolk while inside the mother's body. Young of the other two species feed on secretions from the lining of the mother's oviduct.

Both larval and adult salamanders are carnivorous. They eat a wide variety of insects, worms, snails, and tadpoles. Large salamanders with wide mouths eat fishes, other salamanders, and small mice. Aquatic salamanders usually suck prey into their mouths. Terrestrial salamanders usually capture prey by slapping the prey with their large, sticky tongues and then jerking the tongues — plus victims — back into their mouths, much as frogs do.

Salamanders protect themselves against predators in many ways. If camouflage doesn't work, some species ooze poisonous secretions. Fire salamanders spray poison from their skin glands when they're attacked. Some salamanders threaten attackers by opening their mouths and lashing their tails. Sometimes the tail-lashing is more than a threat. The salamander oozes a sticky substance that works like glue. Garter snakes that tangle with these salamanders sometimes can't free themselves from their own coils for a day or two!

Many kinds of salamanders can make their tails fall off when grabbed, a behavior called *tail autotomy*. The tail keeps wiggling for a while after it breaks off, and the predator pounces on the tail while the rest of the salamander flees. In time a new tail will *regenerate* (grow back). Tail autotomy, however, costs the salamander something. First, regenerating a new tail uses a lot of energy that otherwise could be spent growing or reproducing. Second, the regenerated tail is usually smaller than the original one. The next time the salamander is attacked, the smaller tail might not divert the predator's attention as well. Third, many salamanders store fat in their tails — energy for a time when food is scarce or when needed to produce eggs. Without its tail, a salamander has lost its reserve.

The largest salamander in the world, the Chinese giant salamander, is the largest living amphibian. Adults can reach 5 feet and weigh nearly 90 pounds. The Japanese giant salamander reaches a length just a couple of inches shy of 5 feet (Plate 13). The largest salamander in the United States, the hellbender, can grow to 3 feet (Plate 7). All three of these large salamanders are aquatic. The largest terrestrial salamander is the tiger salamander, common in many parts of the United States. A big individual can reach 13 inches. Some Mexican lungless salamanders are about an inch long.

Order Gymnophiona: Caecilians

At first glance the third group of amphibians, the caecilians, resemble giant earthworms (Figure 30, Plate 14). Both are slimy, thin, legless creatures. Like earthworms, caecilians' bodies are encircled with grooves. Their tiny eyes are usually covered by a thin layer of skin or bone. The tail is either short or absent. Caecilians have lungs, but in many species the left lung is small or absent.

Caecilians' skin feels slimy because it's covered with mucus. In fact, it's hard to hold onto a squirming caecilian. Some caecilians have small scales beneath the surface of the skin. Frogs and salamanders have no scales at all.

About 186 species of caecilians live in the world's tropical regions: in Asia, Africa, and Central and South America. Most people in the United States have never seen or even heard of

Figure 30. This terrestrial yellow-striped caecilian lives in Cambodia, Laos, Thailand, Myanmar, and Vietnam.

caecilians, because caecilians don't live there. Most species live underground. Fossorial species generally have blunt heads. They use their heads to push and compact the soil while they burrow. Some species are aquatic. These generally have compressed bodies with fins. Although most caecilians are dull gray, brown, or black, some are blue, orange, pink, or bright yellow. Some are plain, others are striped.

Because of their secretive habits, we don't know much about the ecology and behavior of caecilians. Our best guess is that about 80% of all caecilians are oviparous. They lay their eggs either in the water or on land. In some that lay their eggs on land near water, the eggs hatch as larvae that wriggle to water. In others, the eggs undergo direct development. In some species, the female stays with her eggs. Just as with frogs and salamanders, these mothers probably protect the eggs from predators and keep the eggs moist. An estimated 20% of caecilians are viviparous. In these species, the young get nutrients from the mother while developing inside her body. They scrape the lining of the mother's oviduct with their teeth and feed on secretions that ooze out.

Caecilians are the only vertebrates that have tentacles. A caecilian has two tentacles, one on each side of the head, between the eye and the nostril. Because their eyes are fairly useless, caecilians use their tentacles for locating and identifying prey. They taste and smell with their tentacles. When they're not using them, they can withdraw their tentacles back into their heads.

Terrestrial caecilians often eat earthworms. Unlike a frog or salamander, a caecilian doesn't capture prey with its tongue. It slowly moves toward the worm until it can almost touch it, then it strikes and bites with its powerful jaws. The caecilian's long, fang-like, backward-curving teeth hold the worm secure. Aquatic caecilians eat invertebrates, including insect larvae (Figure 31).

Some caecilians can grow to a length of 4 feet. They're slender, though, usually less than 1 inch wide. Many are no more than 10 inches long and less than half an inch wide. The smallest caecilians are about 3 inches long as adults.

Figure 31. Rio Cauca caecilians, from Colombia and Venezuela, are aquatic.

◦◦

Aquatic or terrestrial, oviparous or viviparous, herbivorous or carnivorous, amphibians are fascinating animals. They're the transitional *vertebrates* between the fishes and the reptiles. Most scientists believe that amphibians *evolved* (changed over many, many years) from lobe-finned fishes. These ancient fishes had lungs and strong fins. During dry periods when their ponds dried up, lobe-finned fishes might have crawled about on land in search of water. Over millions of years, fins evolved into legs. Lungs became more efficient. Other changes evolved that allowed early amphibians to make better use of the land.

The earliest amphibian fossils date back to about 360 million years ago. These early amphibians were carnivores that grew to more than 3 feet in length. Amphibians were common in fresh water and on land for the next 70 million years. During this time some forms evolved into early reptiles. Some of the early reptiles eventually gave rise to the dinosaurs. By the time dinosaurs ruled Earth, the number of amphibians had dwindled. Some persisted, however, and eventually evolved into the frogs, salamanders, and caecilians that we know today.

Current-day amphibians are restricted in where they can live. No place too dry or cold will work. Although many amphibians now live on land, they are still very tied to water. They need moist environments because they easily lose water from their skin. Another problem is that because amphibians are *ectothermic*, they become inactive at low temperatures. But these characteristics work to amphibians' advantage as well. They can quickly absorb water through their skin by resting on dew-covered leaves or moist soil. Because they have low energy requirements, they can go for months without food. When it gets too cold, an amphibian hunkers down under a log or rock or goes underground where it stays until the temperature warms.

As you'll see, reptiles are less restricted than amphibians in where they can live.

4

Meet the Reptiles I

The word reptile comes from the Latin word *reptilis* meaning a creeping, crawling animal. There are four groups, or *orders*, in the class Reptilia. We'll look at two orders in this chapter. Turtles and tortoises belong to the order Testudines (also called Chelonia). *Testudines* means "a tortoise shell" in Latin, and Chelonia comes from the Greek word *chelone* meaning "tortoise." Turtles and tortoises are unique among reptiles. They carry their homes — their shells — with them. The order Crocodilia includes crocodiles, gavials (also called gharials), alligators, and caimans. Crocodilia comes from the Latin word *crocodilus* meaning "crocodile." These are the most prehistoric-looking of all the modern reptiles.

Order Testudines: Turtles

Turtles are easy to recognize, thanks to their bony shells that provide instant protection. At the first hint of danger, many turtles draw their legs, tail, and head into the shell and shut out the world. A turtle's shell consists of two parts. The top part is called the *carapace*, and the lower part is called the *plastron* (Figure 32). These two parts are connected by a bony bridge on each side. In most turtles the shell is covered with

Figure 32. The lower part of a turtle's shell is called the plastron.

sturdy *scutes* — plates made from *keratin*. In soft-shelled turtles and leatherback sea turtles, the shell is covered with thick, leathery skin.

About 313 *species* of turtles share the planet with us today. Many live in the ocean and in fresh water, including rivers, streams, ponds, lakes, marshes, and swamps. Some live on land — in forests, deserts, and grasslands. Although most turtles are brown, black, or dull green, some have bright yellow, orange, or red spots or stripes. Some turtles are unusual-looking (Plate 6). All turtles breathe with lungs. Some *aquatic* species also breathe underwater through the skin in their throat and hind-end regions.

What's the difference between a turtle and a tortoise (Figure 33)? Just as with poodles and dogs — and toads and frogs — all tortoises are turtles, but not all turtles are tortoises. Tortoises are certain turtles that live only on land. As you would expect, the feet of aquatic and *terrestrial* turtles are different. Many tortoises have stumpy hind feet, like elephants' feet. Gopher tortoises and Bolson tortoises use their front feet as scoops to dig burrows in the sand. Freshwater turtles have webbed hind feet that allow them to swim efficiently. Sea turtles have flippers for feet, and they use these like oars to paddle through the water. Some sea turtles can swim as fast as our best Olympic swimmers! Box turtles and most other turtles that live on land have high, dome-shaped carapaces. In contrast, painted turtles and most other aquatic turtles have flatter carapaces.

Figure 33. All tortoises are turtles, but not all turtles are tortoises. **Left:** Tortoises live on land, usually have stumpy hind feet, and have high, dome-shaped carapaces. **Right:** Most other turtles, such as this painted turtle, have webbed feet or flippers and flatter carapaces.

Turtles don't have teeth. Instead, their strong, razor-sharp jaws cut and crush their food (Figure 34). Some turtles slurp fish and small *invertebrates* from the water. Other aquatic turtles eat fruits and flowers that fall into the water. Snapping turtles eat just about anything they can swallow — fishes, frogs, snakes, snails, aquatic plants, and other turtles. Green turtles eat seaweed. Leatherback turtles eat jellyfish, composed mostly of water and stinging cells. Hawksbill sea turtles eat sponges, an amazing feat since the skeletons of sponges are made of silica (glass). Some tortoises are strictly *herbivorous* and eat only berries and other fruits, flowers, and leaves. *Omnivorous* tortoises eat both plants and animals such as insects, worms, and slugs.

Figure 34. Turtles don't have teeth, but they have strong jaws.

Figure 35. This box turtle can withdraw so completely and tightly into its shell that it is nearly impossible to pry it open.

Small turtles are food for crabs, fishes, snakes, alligators, birds, and mammals. Killer whales and sharks eat sea turtles. How does a turtle avoid becoming food?

Some, such as box turtles and mud turtles, have hinges in their plastrons (Figure 35). After the turtle withdraws its head, feet, and tail into the shell, it can close the plastron tightly against the carapace. Side-necked turtles don't have this option (Figure 36). The best they can do is bring their head and neck in alongside the body in the gap between the carapace and plastron. This position leaves them partially vulnerable to predators.

Figure 36. Side-necked turtles, such as this snake-necked turtle from Australia, cannot withdraw completely into their shells.

The best defense for an aquatic turtle sunning itself on a log is to dive into the water and swim like crazy. Tortoises often bask at the entrances to their burrows. When they sense danger, they bolt down their tunnels and disappear. Snapping turtles are quick to bite with their strong jaws. Musk turtles are called "stinkpots" for good reason. When threatened, a musk turtle squirts a foul-smelling substance from glands on its thighs.

Turtles communicate with each other primarily during courtship and during aggressive interactions. For some species, vision is important. A turtle may bob its head up and down or side to side. Turtles sometimes open their mouths widely and threaten intruding individuals. Many turtles use smell to identify another individual as male or female. Turtles also communicate by touch. A male might tap or rub a female's head. Sometimes male tortoises vocalize while following females during courtship.

All turtles, whether terrestrial or aquatic, lay their eggs on land. Typically, the female digs a hole in the ground, lays her eggs in the hole, and covers the eggs with dirt (Figure 37). In a few species, the mother simply lays her eggs on the surface of the ground, amidst fallen leaves. Turtles don't take care of their young. Instead, the sun's heat incubates the eggs. After the baby turtles break through their egg shells, they dig their way out of the ground to the surface.

The earliest turtles were around long before the dinosaurs. Their body form must have been a good one, because they haven't changed much in the past 200 million years. Turtles watched the dinosaurs go extinct, but turtles continued living.

Figure 37. This green turtle has hauled her heavy body out of the ocean and up onto the beach. She dug a hole in the sand and is now laying her ping-pong ball shaped, leathery eggs.

Turtles are some of the world's longest-living *vertebrates*. Box turtles can live 50 years. Sea turtles and large tortoises can live as long as the average human. Tortoises can live to 100 years or more in captivity.

Leatherback sea turtles are the world's largest turtles. They can grow to a length of 8 feet and weigh more than 1500 pounds. The world's largest freshwater turtle is the alligator snapping turtle. A full-grown adult can weigh 200 pounds. The largest tortoise is the Galápagos tortoise, which can reach 4 feet and weigh 600 pounds. Adult common bog turtles never get bigger than 4 inches.

Order Crocodilia: Crocodilians

Crocodilians have short, strong legs. Their webbed feet allow them to walk on wet mud without sinking in. Crocodilians often float in the water, with only their eyes and nostrils

Figure 38. My, what big teeth this American crocodile has!

above the surface. These prehistoric-looking reptiles have long snouts, and they breathe with lungs. Cone-shaped teeth fit into sockets in their strong jaws, just as our teeth do (Figure 38). A protective armor of bony plates covers their tough skin. They use their powerful tails for swimming and as whips to defend themselves.

Most crocodilians live in tropical and subtropical regions. In the southeastern United States and in China, however, alligators live a little farther north than the other crocodillians (Figure 39). Most crocodilians live in fresh water, but a few live in slightly salty or even sea water. Crocodilians are excellent swimmers. When they're not in a hurry, they often crawl on

Figure 39. This American alligator appears to be snoozing on a lazy summer afternoon.

their bellies across land. Some lift up their bellies high off the ground and gallop surprisingly quickly on land.

Scientists divide the 23 living species of crocodilians into three groups: (1) crocodiles, (2) gavials, and (3) alligators and caimans.

It's easy to distinguish crocodiles from the other two groups because the long, fourth tooth on each side of the lower jaw fits into a groove in the side of the upper jaw. When the crocodile's mouth is closed, these teeth are exposed, giving the animal a fierce look. Some of the 13 species of crocodiles live in salt water; others live in freshwater streams and rivers.

Figure 40. The bulbous growth at the tip of this male gavial's snout magnifies his hisses — the better to be heard.

The two species of gavials have extremely long and slender snouts, with lots of sharp teeth exposed at the tip (Figure 40). The fourth tooth and all the teeth in front of it rest on the outside of the upper jaw when the mouth is closed. Gavials live in freshwater rivers.

In alligators and caimans, the long fourth tooth on each side fits into a pit in the animal's upper jaw. When the mouth is closed you can't see the tooth. That's why alligators and caimans don't look as mean as other crocodilians. Another difference is that most crocodiles have pointed snouts, while alligators have rounded snouts. All eight species of alligators and caimans live in or near fresh water.

Crocodilians display very active courtship. For example, male alligators bellow loudly and slap their heads against the water surface. This commotion attracts females. A female places her snout on the male's head or snout, and the two rub each other's head and snout for a while. Eventually, if the female is receptive, the animals circle each other in the water and blow bubbles. If the female is not receptive, she growls and swims away.

All crocodilians are *oviparous*. Alligators, caimans, and a few species of crocodiles lay their eggs inside nests that they build by heaping vegetation and soil into a mound. The heat from the sun and rotting vegetation incubates the eggs. Other crocodilians lay their eggs in holes they dig in the ground. Female crocodilians guard their nests and are attentive mothers.

Parental care behavior of the American alligator is just as impressive as that of many birds. The young begin to peep even before they have completely emerged from their eggshells. The mother responds by ripping apart the nest. She gently nudges one or two babies into her mouth and then carries them to water. She repeats the process until all are safely swimming in their new home (Figure 41). The mother and her babies stay together for about two years, while she protects them from predators. Although the young can find their own food, they sometimes eat chunks of food that drop from their mother's mouth while she's eating. She doesn't mind . . . though you better believe she would fight any other alligator that tried to share her meal!

Crocodilians "talk" to each other. Babies peep while still inside their eggs, presumably communicating with each other. *Herpetologists* think this communication may enable the young to hatch at the same time. During the year or two that they stay near their mother, the young and their mother vocalize to each other as a way of staying together. A young responds to danger by peeping, and the mother comes to the rescue. Adult males vocalize also. They bellow loudly during the breeding season, warning intruders not to enter their territories.

Young crocodilians eat insects and frogs. As they grow, they eat fishes, turtles, birds, and mammals. Crocodilians usually feed at night, catching their prey in the water. A crocodilian lies in wait, floating in the water with just its eyes and

Figure 41. This baby alligator made it to the water thanks to its mother. It's amazing that an animal whose jaws are strong enough to crush a human carefully carries her newly hatched babies in her mouth!

nostrils above the surface. Spying dinner, it lunges and grabs the prey in its powerful jaws. If the prey is large, the crocodilian may drown it underwater before eating. If a crocodilian captures an animal on land, it often drags the prey to water to eat it.

A crocodilian doesn't chew its food. It tears the prey into bite-sized chunks and swallows those whole. If a catch is especially large, the crocodilian may wait a day or more to dine until the prey begins to rot. Then it's easier to tear apart. Crocodilians swallow stones, which presumably help to grind and break up bones in their stomachs.

Many types of crocodilians shared Earth with the dinosaurs. Some of these crocodilians were huge. Fossil remains of one found in Texas include a skull nearly 6 feet long. If its body proportions were similar to those of our modern-day crocodilians, this giant could have been 45 feet long — as big as *Tyrannosaurus rex*, the meat-eating "King of the Dinosaurs." This huge crocodilian might have eaten small dinosaurs, perhaps even baby *T. rex*. Like the turtles, crocodilians watched the dinosaurs go extinct and they survived. They haven't changed much through the millions of years since.

The largest crocodilian, the saltwater crocodile, is also the largest living 4-legged reptile. Some giants grow to a length of 24 feet, more than half the length of *Tyrannosaurus rex*. Saltwater crocodiles live over a wide area, from India to northern Australia. People fear this species and the Nile crocodile because they're large and aggressive (Figure 42). They'll eat humans if given the opportunity. The smallest crocodilians are

Figure 42. Nile crocodiles can grow to 18 feet in length. They often ambush prey at the edges of rivers and lakes, drag their victims into the water, and drown them. Then the feast begins.

dwarf caimans, usually less than 4 feet long (Plate 15). They live in streams and pools in rain forests in the Amazon Basin of South America. People swim with these caimans without fear because they're not dangerous to humans.

5

Meet the Reptiles II

The remaining two reptile *orders* are the largest and the smallest groups — based on the number of species they contain. The largest reptile order, the one with the most species, is Squamata, the lizards and snakes. Squamata comes from the Latin word *squamae* meaning "scale." Even though they belong to the same order, we'll consider the lizards and snakes separately because these groups are so large and diverse. The smallest order is Rhynchocephalia — two species of tuatara. Rhynchocephalia comes from the Greek words *rhynchos* and *kephale* meaning "snout" and "head," a name that refers to the wide snout of these lizard-like reptiles.

Order Squamata: Lizards and Snakes

Lizards

Lizards and snakes both belong to the order Squamata, largely based on similarities in their skeletons (Figure 43). What's the difference between the two groups? You'll probably answer, "Of course, lizards have legs and snakes don't!" That's usually, but not always, true. Some burrowing lizards don't have legs. For example, of the 133 *species* of worm lizards, only three have small legs; the rest have no legs at all. These

Figure 43. The order Squamata consists of two major groups: **Top:** lizards, like this transverse anole, and **Bottom:** snakes, like this copperhead.

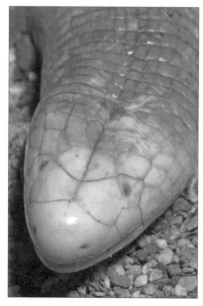

Figure 44. White-bellied worm lizards spend much of their lives in underground burrows.

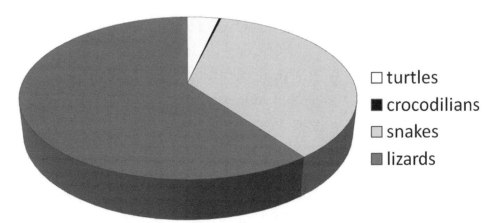

□ turtles
■ crocodilians
□ snakes
■ lizards

Figure 45. Other groups of reptiles dwarf in terms of number of species in comparison to the lizards. Tuatara are not included in this pie diagram because, with only two species, their sliver of the pie wouldn't show up!

lizards have long worm-like bodies, tiny eyes, and no external ears — perfect characteristics for digging underground (Figure 44; Plate 15). Several other, unrelated lizards also burrow underground and lack legs.

Most lizards can blink their eyes because they have moveable eyelids. Snakes lack moveable eyelids. Other differences between lizards and snakes involve organs and bones inside the body — structures you can't see.

There are more species of lizards than of all the other living reptiles combined (Figure 45). The 5247 species of lizards come in an amazing diversity of shapes and sizes, from short and fat to long and skinny. Gila monsters and beaded lizards, both *venomous* lizards, are chunky with short, thick tails (Plate 4). Some slender legless lizards are nearly 50 inches long, two-thirds of which is tail. Skinks have smooth skin. Horned lizards and Australian thorny devils are spiny (Plate 8).

Lizards live almost everywhere in the world except in polar regions. They live in hot deserts, lowland rain forests, wet cloud forests, high mountains, and everywhere in between, though they are most common in warm areas. Regardless of where they live, all lizards breathe with lungs.

Lizards shed their skin from time to time, making room to grow larger (Figure 46). The worn-out skin usually comes off in large pieces, over several days. The new skin is often more brightly colored than the old skin that is about to be shed.

Most lizards are *oviparous*. Females of most species abandon their eggs, but in a few species the female stays with her eggs until after they hatch. Some lizards bury their eggs in the sand, dirt, or under fallen leaves on the ground. Others wedge

Figure 46. This South American gecko is shedding its old skin and revealing a bright, new body.

Figure 47. By spreading his dewlap, this male green anole warns: "Stay away, this is my territory."

their eggs into crevices between rocks or hide them in rotting logs. About 20% of lizards are *viviparous*.

Lizard courtship often involves visual displays that are nearly as complex as those of birds. Males of many species have horns or crests that they show off when trying to attract females. During the breeding season, males of some species become brightly colored. They display these patches of color during courtship.

Often males compete among themselves for opportunities to mate with females. In many species, males defend territories from other males. The advantage in having a territory is that the owner can mate with any female that enters his area. Males defend their territories by using threatening body postures, bobbing their heads, and spreading out their *dewlaps* (throat fans) (Figure 47). Some males do push-ups and show their bright patches of color. If displays don't work, the lizards might bite each other.

For most lizards, the tongue is a critical body part. Whether long or short, rounded or forked, the tongue flicks in and out of its owner's mouth. The tongue picks up chemicals from the ground, prey, or a potential mate. Once back in the mouth, the tongue presses against the roof of the mouth and transfers the chemicals to a sense organ called the *Jacobson's organ.* Some species of lizards rely on their sense of smell more than others. Monitors have long, forked tongues and well-developed Jacobson's organs (Plate 8). Chameleons use their tongues very little, if at all, to explore their surroundings and each other.

Lizards' diets are diverse. Many eat a wide variety of insects. Some eat scorpions. Marine iguanas dive up to 50 feet under the surface of the ocean to munch on seaweed. Young green iguanas eat insects, but as adults they eat leaves, fruits, and flowers. Nile monitor lizards feast on crabs and crocodile eggs. Tokay geckos eat small mice and lizards. Caiman lizards eat only snails, which they crush between their strong jaws. Horned lizards eat mainly ants.

Some lizards simply open their mouths, grab a prey with their jaws, and swallow it whole. Many, however, zap prey with their tongues. Chameleons are especially adept at this — the "sharpshooters" of the lizard world. A chameleon's tongue can shoot out and latch onto an insect that's as far away as two chameleon body-lengths (not counting the tail). Each of the chameleon's eyes swivels independent of the other (Figure 48). The lizard can use one eye to scan for prey to the side and the other eye to scan straight ahead. When one eye spots an insect, the other swings around to focus on it as well. The depth

Figure 48. This wavy chameleon seems to be saying, "I see you!"

perception (ability to judge distances) that both eyes now provide increases the chameleon's chance of zapping the insect.

Gila monsters and beaded lizards have venom glands in the tissue along their lower jaws (Figure 49; Plate 4). Unlike venomous snakes, these lizards don't inject the venom through fangs. Instead, when the lizard bites into a baby bird or other prey, the venom flows into the mouth and seeps into the puncture wounds. Although the venom might help to subdue prey in some cases, many biologists believe that these lizards use their venom mainly to protect themselves.

Even for venomous lizards, often the best defense against predators is simply not to be noticed. Many lizards are *camouflaged*. Once they're noticed, the next defense may be escape. Anoles run up trees. Chuckwallas run into crevices between rocks and gulp air. By inflating their lungs, the lizards become larger. Their bodies get tightly wedged in between the rocks, making it impossible for predators to get to them. A horned

Figure 49. Beaded lizards live from central Mexico to northern Central America.

lizard makes a mad dash for the nearest clump of vegetation. Some desert lizards run, dive into the sand, and disappear. A green iguana or an Asian water dragon basking on a tree branch overhanging a river will drop into the water below. Basilisk lizards from Central and South America escape by running over the water surface on their hind legs. Their feet work as water skis, thanks to fringed scales on the back edges of their toes.

Once caught, many lizards defend themselves. Some bite. Lizards without weapons may bluff by hissing, squeaking, opening their mouths, or inflating their bodies (Plate 10). An Australian frilled lizard has a huge flap of loose skin around its neck that it spreads when bothered. This causes the lizard to look much larger and fiercer than it really is. Some species startle their attackers. Blue-tongued skinks flip out their bright blue tongues. Horned lizards squirt blood from the corners of their eyes. Spinytail geckos spray goo from glands in their tails.

Figure 50. This lava lizard sacrificed its tail to escape from a predator.

As a last resort, a lizard may drop its tail to save its life (Figure 50). When a predator grabs the lizard and the tail drops off, nerve reflexes keep the tail wiggling. If the lizard is lucky, the predator pounces on the tail while the lizard escapes. As with salamanders, a new tail usually grows back, but often it's shorter than the original one and sometimes a different color. Lizards have the same costs to losing and *regenerating* their tails as do salamanders. They drop their tails as a last resort because their tails are valuable body parts. Depending on the species, the tail might grasp onto tree branches, act as a balance while climbing in the trees, serve to balance the lizard's body as it runs, or store fat.

Komodo dragons are the largest lizards (Figure 7; Plate 8). Growing to a length of 10 feet, these lizards live only on five small islands in Indonesia, including Komodo. At the other extreme, some dwarf chameleons of Madagascar and Africa are only an inch long. The smallest lizard is a gecko found on an island off the coast of the Dominican Republic. Its total length, including tail, is barely more than half an inch.

Snakes

About 100 million years ago snakes *evolved* from lizard-like reptiles that had legs. Since then, snakes have lost their legs and developed different ways of moving. The presence of lots of vertebrae — from about 120 to over 400 — helps snakes move without legs and allows them to coil and bend easily (Figure 51). Snakes also have lost the moveable eyelids that most lizards have. Snakes can't blink their eyes. Instead, a

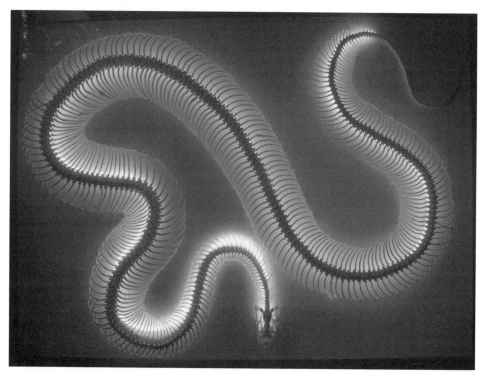

Figure 51. Snakes have LOTS of vertebrae!

transparent scale protects the eye from dirt. Some snakes are brightly colored (Plate 3).

How do all of a snake's internal organs fit into its narrow, tube-like body? For starters, the left lung is either small or absent. Many of the other organs are displaced from their usual positions in other reptiles. For example, the kidneys are not across from each other. One is located more forward than the other.

About 3149 species of snakes live on Earth today. They occur almost everywhere on the continents: in deserts, forests, grasslands, and in fresh water. Although they occur in oceans, snakes are absent from most islands. More species of snakes live in the tropics than anywhere else. Snakes live on the ground, in crevices or underground burrows, in the trees, and in water. Like all other reptiles, snakes breathe with lungs. Sea snakes, however, also breathe underwater through their skin.

Some people assume that all snakes look alike. After all, they all have cylindrical bodies. *Herpetologists* who study snakes, however, are impressed by their diverse appearances. Snakes' bodies range from long and slender, as in vine snakes, to heavy and robust, as in African puff adders. Sea snakes use their flattened tails as oars to paddle through the ocean. Many *arboreal* snakes have huge, bulgy eyes (Figure 52). Burrowing snakes have tiny eyes and are nearly blind.

Like lizards, snakes shed their skins (Figure 53). Instead of peeling off in large patches, however, a snake's skin usually comes off in one piece. Once the old skin begins to peel around

Figure 52. My, what big eyes this blunt-head tree snake has!

Figure 53. A snake, such as this corn snake, sheds its outer layer of skin when it wears out. An active snake might shed six or more times during the year, whereas a less active snake might shed only twice.

the lips, a snake rubs the side of its head on the ground. This folds the skin back, and the snake crawls out of its old skin.

If you watch a snake closely, you'll see its narrow, forked tongue flicking in and out of its mouth (Figure 54). The snake is "tasting" its environment. Each time the tongue flicks out, it picks up chemicals. Flicking back in, the tongue touches the roof of the mouth and — just as lizards do — transfers the chemicals to the Jacobson's organ. This sense organ allows the snake to locate food and mates and to detect predators.

Sensing chemicals by their tongues and Jacobson's organs are the main ways that snakes communicate with others of the same species. Visual signals aren't used much, and snakes can't hear. They can pick up vibrations through whatever they're resting on, however. Some snakes touch during courtship, as when the male rubs his chin against the female or gently bites her.

All snakes are *carnivorous*. Depending on the species, snakes eat ants, termites, grasshoppers, spiders, snails and

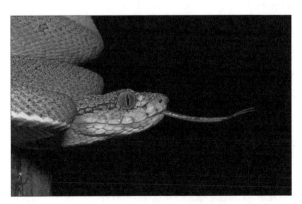

Figure 54. My, what an impressive forked tongue this two-striped forest pit viper has!

slugs, centipedes, crayfish and crabs, fishes, amphibians, lizards, crocodilians, turtles, birds, mice and rats, deer, and the eggs of fishes, frogs, reptiles, and birds. Thus, it's not surprising that snakes capture and handle their prey in many different ways.

Many snakes grab their prey with their jaws, work them into their mouths, and swallow. Boas and pythons coil around their prey and squeeze, or constrict, until the prey suffocates or its heart stops beating. Constriction allows a snake to tackle a large prey with less chance of getting hurt. For example, a 25-foot-long anaconda can constrict and eat a 6-foot crocodilian.

Another way to subdue a victim is to inject it with venom and wait for the animal to die. Substances in the venom soften the prey, allowing the snake to digest its meal faster. Although many venomous snakes use their venom to protect themselves, they mainly use it to subdue prey.

Pit vipers, including rattlesnakes, copperheads, and bushmasters, have pits located just above their mouths, one on each side, between the eye and the nostril (Figure 55). These pits are lined with heat-sensitive cells. A pit viper cruising for a meal can sense heat coming from an animal that's warmer than the surroundings. This method of finding food works especially well for *endothermic* prey — birds and mammals. Most boas and pythons also have heat-sensitive pits. In these snakes, however, the pits are often located along the upper lip (Figure 55).

Snakes often eat prey that are much wider than their heads. How does a snake with a 1-inch-wide head swallow a rat? The key is that a snake's jaws are loosely connected, and

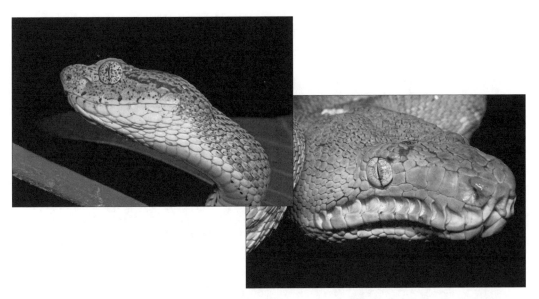

Figure 55. Top: Pit vipers, such as this two-striped forest pit viper, have one heat-sensitive pit on each side of the head, located between the eye and the nostril. **Bottom:** Most boas and pythons, such as this tree boa, have heat-sensitive pits located along the upper lip.

the jaws can be separated into right and left halves. This is very different from a person's jawbone, which is solidly connected in the front. The two parts of the snake's lower jaw can move apart, allowing the snake to open its mouth wider. Once the prey is in its mouth, the snake moves its jaws sideways, first one side then the other until it works the animal down its throat. To understand how this works, imagine putting a pillow into a pillowcase that has shrunk and is a little too small. You would alternate pulling up one side of the pillowcase over the pillow, then the other, until the pillow was completely stuffed inside.

Eastern hognose snakes specialize on eating toads (Figure 56). When attacked, a toad often fills its lungs with air and

Figure 56. This toad looks awfully large for the hognose snake to eat, but the snake got it down with no problem.

bloats itself to a larger size. This makes it harder for a predator to swallow it. Once an eastern hognose snake gets a toad in its mouth, it works the toad into the back of its mouth. There, the snake's elongated rear teeth puncture the toad and release the air. Now the toad is thin enough to be swallowed easily.

Some snakes are oviparous, others are viviparous (Figure 57). Even within a closely related group of snakes both forms of reproduction can occur. Boas and pythons belong to the family Boidae. All pythons lay eggs, but all boas give birth to fully developed young. Some vipers, venomous snakes that belong to the family Viperidae, lay eggs. One example is the bushmaster, the largest viper in the New World. Some other vipers, such as rattlesnakes, are viviparous.

In some species of snakes, males that are ready to mate fight among themselves in the presence of females. Coiled around each other, each tries to pin the other to the ground. Usually the snake that stays on top of its opponent the longest wins and mates with the female. Some snakes fight while lying on the ground. Others raise the front half of their bodies in a vertical position and duke it out, sometimes twisting their necks around each other. They sometimes sway their heads back and forth while facing each other, perhaps as a way of estimating the other's strength or size.

Snakes, like all other animals, have predators. Many snakes blend in with their surroundings. When camouflage doesn't work and a snake has been detected, it usually tries to escape. Some snakes defecate when attacked. Dwarf boas squirt

Figure 57. These baby corn snakes hatching from their eggs are on their own, to find their own prey and protect themselves from becoming food for other predators.

blood from their heads. Some snakes bite their attackers —
and some inject venom. Coral snakes advertise their venomous nature with bright colors (Plate 16). Rattlesnakes warn
with a buzzing sound made by shaking the rattles at the end of
the tail (Plate 16).

Anacondas from South America and reticulated pythons
from Southeast Asia are the largest snakes, growing to more
than 25 feet in length. At 16 feet, the king cobra is the longest
venomous snake in the world. Blindsnakes, some of the smallest snakes, measure only 6 inches in length.

Order Rhynchocephalia: Tuatara

Many people have never heard of tuatara (Figure 58). Although many species of tuatara lived on Earth 200 million
years ago, only two exist today. They live on about 30 small
islands off the coast of New Zealand. Both are considered endangered species. The closest relatives of tuatara are a group
of extinct reptiles that lived at the same time as the dinosaurs.
For this reason, tuatara are often called "living fossils." Tuatara look like lizards, but they're different from lizards in many
ways, especially in their teeth and skulls.

Tuatara have crests of spines running down the centers
of their backs. These crests are much larger in males than in
females. The name tuatara comes from the Maori people native to New Zealand and means "spines on the back." The Maori
do not add an "s" to the end of words to make the plural. So,
although it seems natural to us to refer to tuataras, the plural
is really tuatara.

Figure 58. Tuatara resemble lizards, but they're not. They are the only living relatives of an ancient group of reptiles that were abundant when the dinosaurs ruled Earth.

Tuatara and seabirds share their small islands. Both directly and indirectly, tuatara depend on the birds. Tuatara sometimes share burrows with the birds, or they take over burrows that ground-nesting birds have abandoned. Nesting seabirds are fairly messy, and they leave behind huge quantities of droppings, scraps of food, broken eggshells, and dead baby birds. This garbage attracts insects looking for food. Tuatara gather around these garbage heaps and eat the insects.

They also eat birds' eggs and baby birds. Baby birds are easiest to snag at night when they're asleep, and insects gather around the garbage at night to feed. Thus, tuatara feed mostly at dusk and dawn. One unusual aspect of tuatara behavior is that they're active at much cooler temperatures than are most other reptiles.

Tuatara are also unusual reptiles in that they chew their food. In addition to insects, bird eggs, and baby birds, they eat earthworms, snails, and lizards. If the prey is small, a tuatara will capture it on its tongue, bring it into its mouth, and chew it until it's well-shredded. A tuatara impales larger meals on its large front teeth. After transferring the catch to the back of the mouth, the tuatara chews the animal thoroughly before swallowing it.

These reptiles communicate with each other mainly through visual signals. During courtship, a male becomes darker, elevates his spiny crest, raises the front half of his body high off the ground, and struts toward the female. A male defends his territory by elevating his crest and shaking his head from side to side at an intruding male. Usually the intruder flees. If not, the territory owner opens his mouth wide and then quickly snaps it shut. Then he chases the intruder and may bite him.

Mating is a bit rough in tuatara, as the male sometimes bites the female. Ten to twelve months after mating, the female lays 8 to 15 eggs in her burrow. The eggs develop slowly for about 12 to 15 months before they hatch. This is the longest known incubation time for any reptile.

When they're not eating, tuatara spend much of their time in burrows, either ones they've dug or borrowed. During the day they bask in the sun at the burrow's entrance. Growth rate is very slow. Tuatara don't reach maturity until they're about 20 years old. They live a long time — some for over 70 years. Male tuatara can grow to 2 feet in length. Females are a little smaller.

∽

And so we see why reptiles have long fascinated people. Their appearances and behaviors are intriguing. Some are bizarre and amazing.

Although not as old as amphibians, reptiles go back a long way in time. The earliest fossil remains of reptiles are about 330 million years old. The period of time from about 245 million years to 65 million years ago is often called the Age of Reptiles because these animals were so diverse and abundant

Figure 59. During the Age of Reptiles, tens of thousands of reptile species — from small to huge — lived on Earth. The American alligator is one of only about 8734 species of reptiles living today.

on Earth. Many of the early forms, including dinosaurs, went extinct. Fortunately, some of the others survived (Figure 59).

What would the world be like without amphibians and reptiles? Next we'll look at the critical roles these animals play in their environments.

6
Amphibians and Reptiles Play Key Roles in Ecosystems

No living organism lives in a vacuum. Rather, organisms are interconnected with other organisms and their surroundings in what is called an *ecosystem*. An ecosystem consists of all the organisms that live in a given geographic area as well as the physical and chemical components that affect the organisms. These non-living components include, for example, energy, soil, climate, and nutrients. Lakes, tropical forests, savanna grasslands, mangrove swamps, and oceans are all examples of ecosystems.

Animals change throughout their lives. As they go through the stages of their *life cycles*, their roles in their ecosystem often change. When younger, they might be more important as prey items for predators (baby eagles are preyed on more than are adult eagles). They might change their diet from *herbivorous* to *carnivorous* as they age (tadpoles are herbivorous, frogs are carnivorous). Or, they might go from carnivorous to herbivorous as they age (green iguanas). They might damage plants by eating their leaves when young (caterpillars), but pollinate plants as adults (butterflies).

Because animals with *complex life cycles* have larval stages and adult stages that live in different ecological environments, their roles in ecosystems are complex and varied. For example, dragonfly larvae live in the water. They are voracious predators on tadpoles and aquatic insects such as mosquito larvae. In turn, dragonfly larvae are eaten by fishes, turtles, and aquatic bugs and beetles. Adult dragonflies catch flying insects on the wing — adult mosquitoes, gnats, midges, and other small flies. Adult dragonflies are eaten by frogs, spiders, birds, and bats.

Ecosystem roles are just as varied for tadpoles and adult frogs. When frogs lay their eggs in a pond, they provide high-energy food for *aquatic invertebrates*, snakes, and birds. Algae-eating tadpoles remove nutrients from the water, leaving less for other algae-eating pond occupants. The tadpoles provide food for many of the same predators that eat frog eggs. As the tadpoles grow, they remove more and more nutrients from the water. Because the tadpoles leave the pond after they *metamorphose*, the nutrients are transferred from the aquatic environment to the *terrestrial* environment. There, snake, bird, and mammal predators feast on the frogs (Figure 60). Frogs that avoid getting eaten feast on insects and other invertebrates.

Amphibians and reptiles play key roles in energy flow and nutrient cycling, in both aquatic and terrestrial ecosystems. They serve as important predators on invertebrates and *vertebrates*, and they are critical prey for other animals. Because amphibians and reptiles are *ectotherms*, they efficiently convert food into growth and reproduction. Therefore, much of the food they eat ends up as animal tissue for predators that eat

Figure 60. Frogs are main prey items for many snakes.

them. The energy is not spent to maintain a constant body temperature. Think of amphibians and reptiles as conveyor belts. They transfer energy from invertebrates to *endothermic* predators higher up the *food chain.*

A food chain is a single path of energy flow. Consider a field of weeds. The sun, the primary source of energy for most ecosystems, provides energy for the weeds to grow. A grasshopper munches on a weed. A toad eats the grasshopper (Figure 61). A garter snake eats the toad. Eventually a hawk eats the garter snake. Most animals, though, eat more than one type of food. The complexity results in *food webs* made up of interconnected food chains (Figure 62). In our field, caterpillars eat the same weed that the grasshopper eats. Toads eat caterpillars. Field mice and bluebirds also eat grasshoppers and caterpillars. Garter snakes eat field mice, and hawks eat

Figure 61. Many species of amphibians, such as this Fowler's toad, prey on insects.

both field mice and bluebirds. Copperheads eat toads, field mice, and bluebirds. This is a simple example. The food web in this field is actually much more complicated.

What would happen if Earth lost large numbers of amphibians and reptiles? Animals, plants, and many other organisms would suffer. Loss of one link in a food web affects many components of the web.

What might happen if there were no frogs left to eat mosquitoes and other disease-carrying insects? Many more people in tropical countries would die from malaria and other diseases.

If there were no frogs left to eat insects that damage our crops, we'd be in big trouble. In fact, this happened in India. In areas where huge number of frogs were collected for restaurants,

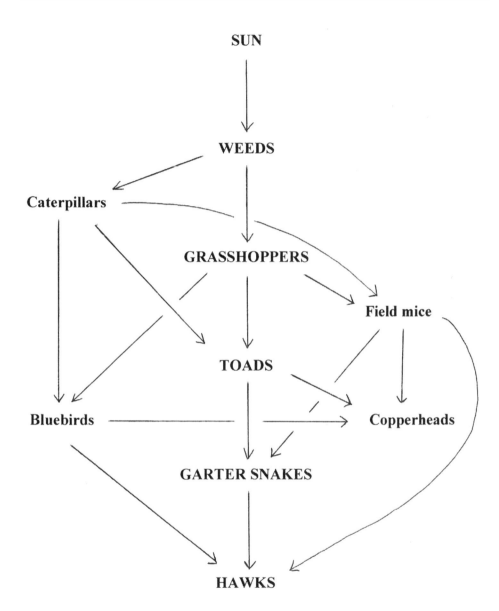

Figure 62. The connected ecosystem components in capital letters, from the sun to hawks, are an example of a food chain. If we add just a few more organisms (those in lower case), we get a complex, interconnected food web. The arrows indicate the direction of energy flow, from the organism consumed to the consumer.

insect pests destroyed crops. Since 1987 India has banned the export of frog legs. The country now appreciates the value of frogs and wants to keep them around.

What if we had no snakes left to eat mammal pests? Again, we'd be in trouble, and it could happen in some places. In the spring, more than 50 towns in Oklahoma, Kansas, Texas, Georgia, New Mexico, Alabama, and Pennsylvania hold "rattlesnake roundups." Rattlesnakes are collected and thrown into pits. Visitors can buy live snakes, dried and mounted specimens, snake meat, skins, heads and rattles made into souvenirs, fat for making snake oil, and gall bladders for Oriental folk medicines. In Oklahoma alone, hunters collect an estimated 10,000 diamondback rattlers for roundups each year. A rattlesnake eats hundreds of rats, mice, and rabbits in its lifetime. When hunters remove thousands of snakes from the countryside, rats, mice, and rabbits multiply in large numbers. Rabbits eat farmers' crops. Rats and mice eat grain and spread disease. Without the snakes to eat these pests, farmers must rely more on pesticides that are both expensive and toxic to the environment.

Gopher tortoises from the southeastern United States provide another good example of the interconnectedness of organisms. These tortoises dig burrows averaging 13 feet long and 6 feet deep with their shovel-like front feet (Figure 63). At least 302 invertebrate *species* and 60 vertebrate species shelter in these burrows. Some of these animals are chance drop-ins. Others, such as the gopher frog, need the burrow's moisture to survive (Figure 64). Gopher tortoises defecate in their burrows. The organic matter attracts feces-eating invertebrates.

Figure 63. This gopher tortoise is making a beeline for the safety of its burrow.

Figure 64. The gopher frog is just one of many animals that live in active gopher tortoise burrows. These frogs also live in abandoned burrows and tunnels made by mammals.

The invertebrates in turn provide food for frog, lizard, and mouse houseguests. Another common resident of gopher tortoise burrows is the eastern indigo snake. The frog, lizard, and mouse houseguests provide gourmet dinners for the indigo snakes. How do the gopher tortoises fit into the food web within their burrows? They make the perfect hosts because they are vegetarians. When gopher tortoise habitat is destroyed and the tortoises disappear, many other organisms are affected as well.

How much longer will amphibians and reptiles be around to serve as critical components of ecosystems? Many species are threatened by the activities of humans. Some species are declining in numbers. Others have gone extinct. The rest of this book is devoted to the causes of these declines and extinctions, and to the ways we can help protect these animals.

7

Disappearing Acts

Silence of the Frogs. Amphibians Out On a Limb. The Mystery of the Vanishing Frogs. The Case of the Disappearing Frogs. Frog Population Leaps Downward. Articles with these and similar titles have appeared in newspapers and magazines for over two decades. What's happening? *Species* and *populations* of amphibians are disappearing. Before going further, we need to focus on the words "species" and "population."

A species consists of all the individuals that could breed with one another if they were all in the same place, but they could not breed with individuals of other species. For example, green treefrogs (*Hyla cinerea*) from a pond in Florida could breed with green treefrogs from a pond in North Carolina, if only they could get together. The Florida green treefrogs could not, however, breed with squirrel treefrogs (*Hyla squirella*) in the same Florida pond. The green treefrogs in the Florida and North Carolina ponds belong to one species, but to different populations. A population consists of individuals of a species that actually do live together and have the opportunity to mate with one another. A species may consist of many different populations each separated from one another, or of only one population.

In the United States, populations of western toads have declined or disappeared from the Rocky Mountains, the Sierra

Nevada Mountains, and the Cascade Mountains. Many populations of red-legged frogs have disappeared from California and Oregon (Figure 65). Populations of cricket frogs have declined or disappeared from the Midwest. All over the country, from New York and New Jersey to California, populations of tiger salamanders have declined or disappeared. Ditto for populations of southern dusky salamanders from South Carolina and Florida. These are just a few examples.

So many amphibians around the world seemed to be in trouble by 1990 that *herpetologists* met to discuss the problem. The scientists vowed to survey more areas to determine the extent of amphibian declines, investigate the possible

Figure 65. Red-legged frogs are listed as threatened on the United States Endangered Species list. Beginning with the California gold rush of 1849 and continuing into the early 1900s, people killed hundreds of thousands of these frogs for food. Since then, escaped introduced bullfrogs have eaten many red-legged frogs. Loss of habitat has taken its toll on the frogs as well.

causes, and educate the public about the problem. Since then, we've spent a lot of time, energy, and money on these three goals.

The International Union for the Conservation of Nature and Natural Resources (IUCN) monitors the *conservation* status of living organisms worldwide. IUCN maintains a catalog of species that face a high risk of extinction. This catalog, called the IUCN Red List of Threatened Species, is updated at least once each year. Scientists evaluate species and give each a designation. Those species of most concern, from those already extinct to those considered to be vulnerable to extinction, are designated as:

- Extinct
- Extinct in the wild
- Critically Endangered
- Endangered
- Vulnerable

The IUCN Red List is our best source of information on the conservation status of species, but not all species are evaluated. For the 2010 list, 95% of amphibian species were evaluated versus only 18% of reptile species.

According to the 2010 Red List, 30% of amphibian species evaluated are threatened with extinction. See Table 1 for the breakdown of designations, from extinct to vulnerable.

To put amphibians' threat in perspective, consider the following. All species of birds and mammals were evaluated for

Table 1. Conservation Status of Amphibians [1]

Total number of amphibian species	6638
Total number of species evaluated	6285
Extinct	37
Extinct in the Wild	2
Critically Endangered	486
Endangered	754
Vulnerable	655

[1] Data from the IUCN 2010 Red List. The total number of amphibian species used by IUCN is a little lower than the currently recognized number of species: 6714.

the 2010 Red List. Twelve percent of birds are considered to be threatened with extinction, and 21% of mammals are considered to be threatened with extinction. Nearly half of all *vertebrate* species were evaluated. Twenty-one percent of all vertebrates evaluated are considered to be threatened with extinction. Clearly amphibians, at 30%, are in trouble. Since the year 1600, 37 species of amphibians have gone extinct. Another two are extinct in the wild. They survive only in captivity.

Amphibians are declining worldwide, from high in the mountains to low deserts and rain forests. Six main causes of amphibian declines have been identified. In some cases, the cause of a particular population decline is still a mystery. Newspaper articles, magazine stories, and radio and television reports about declining and disappearing amphibians appear frequently and inform the public about the problem. We'll look briefly at these six causes here and focus on them in greater detail later.

Habitat destruction or modification is the number one cause of amphibian declines (Figure 66). Cutting down a rain forest and converting it to pasture for cattle destroys homes for amphibians. Filling in a swamp with dirt eliminates breeding sites for frogs and salamanders.

A *parasitic* fungus that attacks amphibians' skin is a second major cause of declines. This fungus has killed amphibians on all continents except Antarctica, which has no amphibians.

Figure 66. A new road being made in the jungle of eastern Ecuador will allow for oil exploration and create more habitat destruction.

Environmental contamination also affects amphibians. Many pollutants that enter the soil, water, and air stunt amphibians' growth and development, cause deformities, or affect reproduction. Others kill. Contaminants range from elements such as mercury to oil runoff on highways to chemicals in fertilizers and pesticides.

Some amphibian populations are declining because people collect too many of these animals. We collect amphibians for food, pets, research, skins, and for folk and modern medicine.

Global climate change might affect amphibians in many ways. High temperatures can kill amphibians. Drought affects their breeding activity. If amphibians don't get enough moisture, they die. Warmer and/or drier conditions change the abundance and availability of amphibians' insect prey. Changing climatic conditions can stress amphibians and make them more vulnerable to parasites and disease.

For centuries, people have introduced animals into places the species don't normally live. Some of these introductions have been on purpose. Cane toads were brought into Australia from South America in 1935 to eat beetles and other damaging insects in the sugar cane fields (Figure 67). Some introductions have been accidental. Rats — often as stowaways on ships — have been introduced accidentally to many places in the world. Regardless of whether the introduction was purposeful or accidental, introduced species might eat native amphibians, or they might compete with them for space or food. They might bring in diseases or parasites.

Figure 67. Cane toads, also called marine toads, were introduced into Queensland, Australia, to eat beetles that feed on sugar cane. The toads didn't stay in the cane fields, however. Since they were introduced in 1935, the toads have dispersed throughout Queensland and into neighboring provinces.

Two tragic amphibian losses are the gastric brooding frogs from Australia. One species was discovered in 1973 but hasn't been seen since 1981. Discovered in 1984, the second species was last seen the following year. These frogs were unique. In both species, the female swallowed her eggs (up to 24) and then brooded the tadpoles in her stomach. After the tadpoles *metamorphosed* into miniature frogs, the mother belched them back up. These were the only animals in the world known to brood their young in their stomachs.

Scientists discovered that the tadpoles released a substance that stopped the mother's stomach from producing digestive acids, thus preventing her from digesting her babies. While the tadpoles were in their incubator — for at least eight weeks — the mother didn't eat. After the froglets emerged, the mother's stomach produced acids again and she could eat. Medical researchers had planned to study these frogs. They hoped that gastric brooding frogs could teach us something about shutting down production of digestive acids, perhaps leading to remedies for stomach ulcers in humans. By the time the researchers had planned their studies, though, the frogs had disappeared.

In some places, many amphibians seem to be in trouble at once. In the Yosemite area of California at least five species of frogs that used to be common in the early 1900s are now hard to find. In certain areas of Australia, populations of numerous species are declining or disappearing. In these and other cases of many species going downhill at once, scientists worry that something serious is wrong with the local environment, but it's hard to say just what that is.

Some scientists have suggested that amphibians might be good indicators of the general health of the environment. Their global decline might signal environmental deterioration that eventually might affect other organisms as well. These scientists have suggested that amphibians might be like the canaries that coal miners used as early warning systems in the mineshafts. Poisonous gases frequently collected in the mineshafts and made the air unsafe for the miners to breathe. Miners took caged canaries down with them because the birds were more sensitive to the fumes than the miners were. As long as the canaries were fine, the miners knew the air was safe for them. If the canaries died, the miners evacuated.

We now know that amphibians do not make good "canaries in a coal mine." They do not provide us with an early warning signal of environmental problems. The decline or disappearance of an amphibian population simply indicates that "something" affected that population in a negative way. But that "something" might not affect other species of amphibians or any other species of animal, including humans.

Reptiles also are declining and disappearing. Some herpetologists argue that reptiles are declining even faster than amphibians and that snakes are disappearing faster than any other group of vertebrates.

Recall that only 18% of all reptile species were evaluated for the 2010 IUCN Red List. Of the species evaluated, IUCN considers 28% to be threatened with extinction. See Table 2 for the breakdown of designations, from extinct to vulnerable. Since the year 1600, 20 species of reptiles have gone extinct. Another one is extinct in the wild. Of these 21 species, 20 lived only on islands. These extinct reptiles include tortoises, geckos, iguanids, other lizards, burrowing boas, and several other snakes.

The same six factors thought to cause amphibian declines also affect reptiles: habitat destruction and modification, over-collecting, introduced species, pollution, disease, and climate change. Again, we'll take a quick look here and focus on these factors in more detail later.

Loss of suitable habitat is the number one cause of reptile declines. Many aquatic reptiles depend on the same wetlands as

Table 2. Conservation Status of Reptiles [1]

Total number of reptile species	9084
Total number of species evaluated	1672
Extinct	20
Extinct in the Wild	1
Critically Endangered	93
Endangered	148
Vulnerable	226

[1] Data from the IUCN 2010 Red List. The total number of reptile species used by IUCN is a little higher than the currently recognized number of species: 8734.

amphibians. In South Carolina, more than 90% of Coastal Plain Carolina bay wetlands have been modified or eliminated. Black swamp snakes, eastern green water snakes, and chicken turtles live mainly in seasonal wetlands. They have little suitable habitat left. Humans are filling in bogs in the eastern United States. Bog turtles are disappearing because their habitat is being destroyed. Ninety-seven percent of longleaf pine habitat in the southeastern United States has been lost. Gopher tortoises, eastern indigo snakes, and eastern diamondback rattlesnakes that lived in these areas have declined.

People have over-collected some reptiles. One example is the giant Galápagos tortoise (Figure 68). The Galápagos Islands sit on the equator, in the Pacific Ocean 600 miles west of the coast of Ecuador. Beginning in the 1500s, whalers, buccaneers, and explorers who visited these islands severely reduced or wiped out entire populations of Galápagos tortoises. Sailors commonly loaded up to 400 tortoises at a time onto their ships. Because the tortoises could be kept alive for a long time, the sailors could have fresh meat for many months. In total, they took more than an estimated 100,000 tortoises for food.

Introduced species have caused declines. For example, several kinds of iguana lizards have disappeared from some of the South Pacific islands where house cats have been introduced. Goats and pigs that people have brought onto the islands destroy so much of the vegetation, both by eating and by trampling it, that lizards have a hard time hiding from the cats.

Figure 68. Galápagos tortoises have seriously declined over the past few centuries due to direct and indirect effects of people. Whereas once there were over 300,000 tortoises, there are only about 15,000 left now.

Some reptiles are negatively affected by environmental pollution. In some cases, contaminants cause genetic changes. Some chemicals accumulate in reptiles' tissues and cause sex changes.

Reptiles contact lethal diseases. A contagious respiratory ailment caused by a bacterium is the likely cause of desert tortoise declines in the southwest United States and of gopher tortoises in the southeast of the country. A viral disease affects green turtles, reducing their ability to see, move, and eat.

Climate change affects reptiles. If temperatures become too warm, vulnerable species might die. Furthermore, the sex of crocodilians, many turtles, and some other reptiles is determined not by genetics, but by the temperature the embryos experience while developing in the nest. At some temperatures, only females are produced. At other temperatures, only males are produced. The range of temperature that produces about 50% of each sex is fairly narrow. What will happen in a warmer world? Will the sex ratio become so skewed toward one sex over the other that individuals can no longer find mating partners?

Why might some amphibians and reptiles decline or go extinct while others survive? Certain characteristics make some species more prone to declines. Consider the following:

Complex Life Cycles. Most amphibians have *complex life cycles*, meaning they pass through a distinct change in body shape. Complex life cycles often involve a change in habitat. In the case of amphibians, this change is usually from water to land. They're exposed to double jeopardy. If there's a problem with either environment, they might not survive. A population of toads that lays eggs in a polluted pond will not survive long even if the woods are still fine for the adults.

Highly Permeable Skin. Amphibians have highly *permeable skin*, which means that substances can enter and pass back out through the skin easily. As mentioned in Chapter Three, this is both an advantage and a disadvantage. The advantage is that amphibians can absorb water through their skin just by sitting on wet leaves or mud. The disadvantage is that water passes back out, so amphibians dry out easily. If the climate changes and becomes drier, they might die. Toxic chemicals from the air, water, and soil can easily enter their bodies and poison them. Species with the most permeable skin might be most vulnerable to drying conditions and to toxins.

Large Body Size. People's activities often affect large animals more than small ones. If hunters kill 50 large boas for their skins, the population is more likely to go extinct than if collectors remove 50 small wormsnakes from the same area to sell as pets. Many fewer boas than wormsnakes likely lived in that area, simply because of the size difference. Larger animals generally need more space than do smaller ones. Thus, a given area can support fewer individuals of a large species as compared to a small one. Said another way, large animals tend to have lower *population densities* (number of individuals per area) than do small animals.

Long Lives. Some snakes live for over 20 years, and some tortoises live for 50 to 80 years or even longer. Some crocodilians and tuatara live for over 70 years. The problem is that these

Figure 69. Both male and female red-backed salamanders establish territories under rocks and logs, and they don't stray far from their homes.

long-lived reptiles don't reproduce very quickly. Many of them take a long time to reach reproductive maturity, and then they only breed every two to four years. In order to reach the age when they can reproduce, these reptiles must survive not only many years of predators, but also many years of environmental and human-caused threats.

Poor Dispersal Abilities. Some amphibians, especially small salamanders, don't move around much. Red-backed salamanders often move less than 2 feet in a day (Figure 69). They don't even move around much within their lifetimes. What would happen if their habitat were polluted or converted to a parking lot? The salamanders wouldn't be able to disperse (move away) far enough to find suitable habitat elsewhere. They would die.

Restricted Distribution on Continents. Many reptiles and amphibians live only in a particular area or region. Imagine a frog species that lives only in forest-bordering streams on one mountain, at an elevation of 3500 feet. It tolerates only a narrow range of temperatures, and it feeds only on insects found near those streams. A mining company pollutes the streams and all the frogs die. Because there was only one population, there are no frogs left to repopulate the area. The species has now gone extinct.

Island Populations. Species that live on islands often have few natural predators, and over time they lose the ability to deal with predators. Therefore, island species are especially vulnerable to introduced predators such as house cats, rats, and dogs.

Colonial Nesting Habits. Reptiles that gather in large groups to lay their eggs are called *colonial nesters*. In some sea turtles, over just a few days, thousands of females clamber out of the ocean and drag themselves onto the beach to lay their eggs. All this activity attracts predators. Raccoons and dogs dig up the eggs and eat them. People, even more efficient than dogs and raccoons, dig up the eggs by the thousands and sell them for food. Sea turtle eggs are considered a delicacy almost everywhere in the world.

Migratory Behavior. Animals that migrate long distances have their own set of problems (Figure 70). Even if a species is protected in one country, it may not be protected in other countries. Green turtles are protected in Australia, but when they migrate to Indonesia people kill them for their meat and collect their eggs. Any species that migrates is potentially exposed to

Figure 70. Green turtles migrate long distances between their nesting and foraging sites. For example, individuals that nest on Ascension Island in the South Atlantic Ocean, about halfway between the coasts of Brazil and Africa, swim over 650 miles to the coast of Brazil to forage on seagrasses.

a wider range of threats than a non-migratory species. A migratory species might have to swim through polluted waters or travel through forests disturbed by humans. Even animals that migrate less than a mile to breeding sites might need to cross highways and risk being squashed by vehicles.

Amphibians and reptiles are disappearing, but does it matter?

8
Why Should We Care?

Some people ask, "Why should I care if amphibians and reptiles disappear? Extinction is a natural process, isn't it?" That's a valuable question. Extinctions have occurred ever since the beginning of life on Earth. *Species* form, go through many changes through time, and die out naturally. These are called natural extinctions. Scientists estimate that over 99% of all life that ever existed on Earth has gone extinct.

Everyone knows about dinosaurs, but no human being has ever seen one alive. The last dinosaurs died out about 65 to 70 million years ago. They weren't the only animals to go extinct about this time, though. Along with them went the large flying reptiles, the swimming reptiles, and many smaller animals. This was a mass extinction. Some scientists believe that these extinctions were gradual, happening over millions of years. One theory is that perhaps the dinosaurs and other animals couldn't cope with changes in the weather that were caused by a large asteroid that crashed into Earth in what is now the Gulf of Mexico.

Extinctions happening now are different. Scientists estimate that current extinctions occur at a rate at least 1000 times faster than most that happened in the distant past. Humans cause most current extinctions, either directly or indirectly.

Some experts believe that an average of at least one species of plant or animal disappears each day.

Many thousands of organisms will go extinct within your lifetime. Some will be amphibians and reptiles (Figure 71). In most cases these won't be natural extinctions. Instead, they'll happen because people are taking those animals' homes, their food, and their lives.

We should care about present-day extinctions because we cause most of them. In 1950, an estimated 2.5 billion people lived on Earth. Sixty-one years later, in 2011, the number had risen to nearly 7 billion. The numbers are predicted to keep rising. The more people on Earth, the more demands we put on the environment and the more we threaten the existence of

Figure 71. The Kihansi spray toad, which lived only in a wetland spray meadow along the Kihansi River Gorge in Tanzania, is now extinct in the wild. A dam built on the river cut off 90% of the water. The wetland dried up. There are some Kihansi spray toads living in zoos, but will they ever be able to go home?

other species. Present-day extinctions are different from past ones because many can be prevented. Humans may be the problem, but we can also be the solution. That's why we should care.

From a scientist's point of view, we should care about the disappearance of amphibians and reptiles because we're still learning about these animals — what they eat, how they defend themselves against predators, how they take care of their young, and how they cope with changing environments. Every year we discover new species, especially from areas that haven't been thoroughly explored. Amphibians and reptiles are fascinating, and we should want them around so that we can learn more about them.

A selfish reason we should care about the health of amphibian and reptile *populations* is that we use these animals for our benefit: medical research, educational purposes, food, and leather. Many people also keep amphibians and reptiles as pets. These animals inspire people all over the world, through our religion, folklore, art, music, and literature. When we lose amphibians and reptiles, we lose part of our culture.

Another reason we should care is that amphibians and reptiles are critical components of *aquatic* and *terrestrial ecosystems* (Figure 72). As discussed in Chapter Six, the world would be a very different place without these animals. You might not think that tadpoles are as important as tigers. Or pythons as important as pandas. The role an animal plays, though, doesn't depend on its size, how cute and fuzzy it is, or how charismatic it is. All animals are valuable links in the web of life.

Figure 72. What would we do without rodent-eating rattlesnakes?

Ethics is a final reason to care about the future of amphibians and reptiles. Central to the value system of most religions and philosophies is the belief that every living species has a right to exist. We are obliged to respect and conserve all of nature, even the species we don't like. In 1982, the United Nations General Assembly adopted The World Charter for Nature. Over 100 nations signed the charter. The charter states: "Every form of life is unique, warranting respect regardless of its worth to man, and, to accord other organisms such recognition, man must be guided by a moral code of action."

What do we mean by conserving nature? The word conserve comes from two Latin words — *servare*, meaning "to guard" or "keep safe," and *con*, meaning "together." *Conservation* is the protection and careful use of a natural area, plant, animal, or other natural resource to make sure it's still around far into the future.

Next we'll look at some of the reasons why amphibians and reptiles are disappearing.

9
We're Taking Too Many

One reason that some amphibians and reptiles are declining or disappearing is that people are collecting too many of them. Unfortunately for them, these animals have beautiful skins, are good to eat, make interesting and exotic pets, are believed to be powerful ingredients in folk and modern medicines, or are useful in teaching and research.

International buying and selling of amphibians and reptiles is big business. The value of these animals and their products imported into the United States every year is hundreds of millions of dollars. Live animals, mostly for the pet trade, account for a small part of this. Most of the money is in products: frog legs for human consumption, and skins and manufactured items such as shoes, boots, and purses.

Skins and Souvenirs

Not all leather comes from cows. Believe it or not, people use frog skin to make shoes, purses, belts, and key cases, and for binding small books. Frog skin makes an alluring covering for artificial fishing bait — or at least fish seem to think so. Toad skins make unusual change purses and shoes (Figure 73). Crocodilian leather is expensive: $600–$800 for a pair of

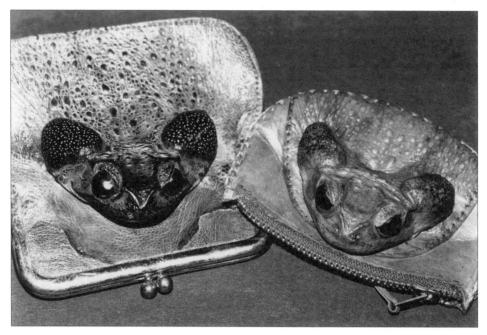

Figure 73. Two marine toads were killed to make these unusual change purses. Would you buy them?

shoes, $300 for a belt, and $1500–$3000 for a purse. Buttons covered with snake skin appeal to some people.

Many *species* of boas, pythons, crocodilians, and lizards are declining because they're heavily hunted for their skins. Boa constrictors and reticulated pythons are made into shoes. Tegu lizards, large terrestrial lizards that can reach 2 to 3 feet in length, are made into cowboy boots. The numbers of reptile skins legally bought and sold each year vary depending on supply and demand, but on average the reported number is about 10 million skins sold by one country and bought by another. The figure would be much larger if we added all the smuggled skins. The main countries that sell reptile skins are the United States, Argentina, Indonesia, and Malaysia. The main countries that buy the skins (to make into shoes and other articles) are Singapore, the United States, Italy, France, and Spain.

Have you seen combs and eyeglass frames that are mottled brown, yellow, black, and reddish brown? They're called "tortoiseshell," but most are plastic. Real tortoiseshell comes from the *scutes* of hawksbill sea turtles, not tortoises (Figure 74). These scutes have beautiful patterns of amber, reddish-brown, blackish-brown, and yellow. In the 8th century, the Japanese began carving tortoiseshell into ceremonial bridal combs. Now they mainly carve tortoiseshell into jewelry, tie clips, and bowls. Until the early 1600s the crafts were made almost

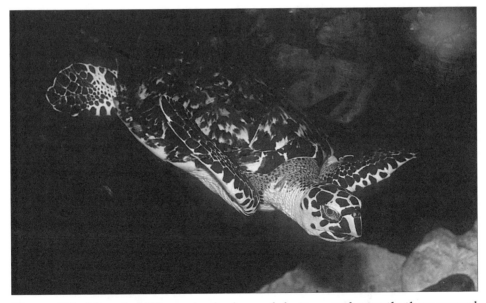

Figure 74. A hawksbill's scutes look much better on the turtle than carved into jewelry or eyeglass frames.

exclusively for the upper class of people. They are still considered a luxury.

Many amphibians and reptiles, or their body parts, are made into souvenirs. Rattlesnake rattles and the heads of hatchling crocodilians, crocodilian teeth, claws, and feet are made into key chains. Toads, iguanas, and turtles are dried, stuffed with cotton, fitted with glass eyes, and varnished (Figure 75).

Food

If you needed to hunt to feed yourself, how would you decide which animals to hunt? You would want the animals to taste good, be fairly easy to catch, and provide a good source of protein. Unfortunately for many species of amphibians and reptiles, they meet all three of these criteria.

Figure 75. In Mexico, Central America, and South America, stuffed toads playing billiards or musical instruments are sold in tourist shops.

People who hunt to feed themselves or their families usually don't kill many animals. Commercial hunters, however, slaughter huge numbers of animals to sell for profit. Most of these animals are shipped to cities or foreign countries. Gourmet dishes include stir-fried frog legs smothered with oyster sauce, frog legs teriyaki, giant bullfrog chop suey, stuffed alligator steaks, poached alligator tail, turtle goulash, iguana stew, and baked gopher snake.

Frog legs are especially popular. With a body length of 7 to 8 inches, a bullfrog has big, muscular legs! During the first half of the 20th century, so many people craved frog legs, and the prices were so high, that hunters in Florida earned up to $500 per day catching frogs. Now we import many of the frog legs eaten in the United States, up to 2000 tons each year. In France, 3000 to 4000 tons of frog legs are eaten each year. Most frog legs eaten in the world are imported from Indonesia and Bangladesh. Asia exports about 200 million pairs of frog legs each year, mostly to the United States, Europe, and Australia.

People also eat salamanders. The axolotl, an *aquatic* salamander from Mexico, in a sense never grows up. Instead of *metamorphosing* from an aquatic larva to a *terrestrial* adult, it keeps its larval features, including its gills, throughout its adult life and stays in the water. Chinese giant salamanders are the world's largest salamanders, at 5 feet long. People have long eaten — and still eat — both of these salamanders. Would you eat an axolotl tamale? Or a Chinese giant salamander steak?

Central Americans have eaten green iguanas and spiny-tailed iguanas for centuries. Now, professional iguana hunters

Figure 76. These live green iguanas are for sale in a market in Nicaragua, Central America. Their legs are tied so that they can't escape.

capture the lizards and ship them to cities (Figure 76). People eat them not only because they taste good (like chicken), but also because they believe the lizards will improve their health. Eggs that are still in the female's body are considered a delicacy.

Over half of Asia's freshwater turtles are heavily hunted for food and are in danger of extinction. The meat is a luxury food, often six times more expensive than chicken or lamb. To impress guests, turtle is the meat of choice. The Chinese have eaten so many turtles from their own country that it's hard to find turtles there anymore. Now the Chinese import turtles from Bangladesh, Pakistan, India, and Nepal. Each year in China an estimated 12 million turtles are sold for their meat.

PLATE 1

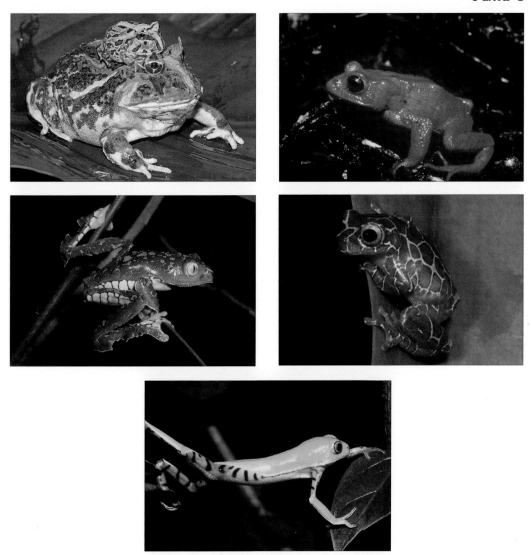

Top left: Brazilian horned frogs — adult or juvenile — are sit-and-wait predators. They sit half-buried among fallen leaves on the ground. When a frog, lizard, or mouse wanders by, the frog opens its mouth and gulps down the unsuspecting prey.

Top right: The last golden toad was seen in 1989. The species used to live in elfin forest near the continental divide in the Cordillera de Tilarán, Costa Rica. This individual is a male. Females were mottled black, yellow, and scarlet.

Middle left: Notice the edges of this South American frog's hind legs. No wonder it's called the fringe leaf frog.

Middle right: This treefrog from Ecuador looks like someone went wild with a paintbrush!

Bottom: This orange-legged leaf frog from Ecuador has orange flanks with dark purple stripes that serve as flash coloration. One species of leaf frog has cream flanks with brown spots. Some leaf frogs have pink or orange spots on a lighter background.

PLATE 2

Top: Although some salamanders are widespread, the Sierra Nevada Ensatina is found only in the Sierra Nevada Mountains of California.

Bottom: When threatened, red salamanders hide their heads and slowly wave their tails in the air. These salamanders secrete mildly toxic substances from skin glands. Some scientists have suggested that red salamanders mimic other species of red-colored salamanders that are even more toxic.

PLATE 3

Top left: In sunlight, the scales of rainbow boas give off iridescent hues of green, blue, and purple.

Top right: Wagler's sipo, a neotropical racer, is a fast-moving snake that eats mostly frogs.

Middle left: The eyelash bush viper from Tanzania, Africa, has one to three hornlike scales above each eye. It is a relatively small viper, reaching about 20 inches in length.

Middle right: Young copperheads are tricksters. When they wiggle their yellow tail tips, nearby frogs approach to eat the "prey." Instead, the snakes grab and eat the frogs.

Bottom: If a predator threatens a mud snake, the snake hides its head under a coil of its body. After all, the head is a critical body part! If needed, the snake stabs the attacker with the tip of its tail.

PLATE 4

Top left: Sky blue and forest green, this Malagasy carpet chameleon is a beauty!

Top right: Thin tree iguanas from Chile spend much of their days foraging for insects on tree trunks.

Bottom left: The genus of this lizard, *Polychrus*, means many-colored. This many-colored bush anole from Ecuador lives up to its name.

Bottom right: Gila monsters live in the deserts of the southwestern United States and northern Mexico, where they eat bird and reptile eggs and nestling mammals and birds. These lizards spend about 95% of the year underground or in shelters. They often fast for months at a time, surviving on fat stored in their tails. When they eat, they can consume more than one-third of their body mass. That would be comparable to a 70-pound person eating 15 large pizzas — at one sitting!

PLATE 5

Top: Surinam toads look as though someone stepped on them. Tiny, beadlike eyes perch on top of their triangular heads. Flaps of skin dangle from the corners of their mouths. These aquatic frogs use their fingers to sift through the mud and sweep invertebrates and small fish into their mouths.

Bottom: This egg-brooding horned treefrog from Ecuador eats other frogs and large insects. When disturbed, the frog opens its mouth and exposes a bright yellow-orange inside. Just to see what would happen, once I put my little finger into the open mouth. The frog snapped her jaws shut in a viselike grip. She nearly punctured my finger and left it throbbing. These frogs use their teeth to hold onto prey that are nearly as long as they are.

PLATE 6

Top left: Matamata turtles live in muddy slow-moving rivers, streams, and swamps in tropical South America. They often stand in shallow water and use their tubular snouts as snorkels to breathe.

Top right: Instead of a bony carapace, a softshell turtle's shell is covered with leathery skin.

Bottom: What a face! This six-tubercled river turtle lives in the Amazon drainages of Colombia, Peru, and Brazil. It eats both aquatic plants and fish.

PLATE 7

Top left: Texas blind salamanders live in water-filled caves. Although blind, these salamanders are active predators. They locate their food by sensing differences of water pressure among waves created by small invertebrates moving about in the water.

Top right: Lesser sirens live in shallow water. They use their external gills throughout life for breathing, but they also use lungs. When the water dries up, they burrow into the mud and form cocoons. They can stay in their cocoons for up to a year. These salamanders have only a pair of small front legs, none in the back. In addition to worms, lesser sirens eat snails, freshwater clams, insects, tadpoles, salamander larvae, and small fish.

Bottom: Hellbenders, with their wrinkles and extra folds of skin, may not be the most attractive salamanders, but they are not aggressive or poisonous as folklore would have us believe. Other common names for hellbenders include snot otter, devil dog, and mud devil. Hellbenders rarely leave the rivers and large streams where they live. Typical of many amphibians, this individual is eating its shed skin.

PLATE 8

Top left: As if its horns and spines aren't enough defense, when a Texas horned lizard is molested by a fox, coyote, or dog, it squirts a fine stream of blood from either or both eyes — up to four feet away! The blood probably tastes bad to these predators, because they shake their heads and salivate when they get the blood in their mouths.

Top right: Male Jackson's chameleons from east Africa have three horns on their heads. These chameleons range up to 13 inches in length and resemble miniature *Triceratops*. When rival males interact, they engage in head-to-head combat by ramming each other with their horns.

Bottom: Komodo dragons are the world's largest lizards. They can weigh more than 200 pounds and grow to 10 feet in length. They have deadly bacteria in their saliva, and they can kill water buffalo for dinner. Nonetheless, some individuals raised in captivity are gentle giants. Smaug, a resident at the Houston Zoo, is tongue-flicking his keeper, Judith, no doubt gaining chemical information about her.

PLATE 9

Top: Female green tree frogs can hear the calls of males of their own species up to about 325 feet away.

Middle left: The Puerto Rican coquí has two parts to its call: "co-quí." The "co" seems to say "This is my calling site," as other males respond to it. Females respond to the "quí" part.

Middle right: This gray tree frog belting out his "love song" is perched on the stem of a horsetail.

Bottom: Argentine common toads call from shallow water. If he's successful in attracting a female, he will fertilize her little black eggs — up to 5000 of them.

Plate 10

Top: What a face! The completely aquatic Lake Titicaca frog does most of its breathing through its skin. Baggy folds of skin provide extra surface area for absorption of oxygen.

Bottom: Veiled chameleons, as is true of many reptiles, open their mouths and hiss when frightened, disturbed, or picked up. They're communicating, "Don't mess with me!"

PLATE 11

Top: When I tried to take this Darwin's frog's picture, it flipped over and played dead. Maybe it thought I wanted to eat it!

Bottom: When disturbed, American toads often crouch and stay still. If a predator attacks, it gets toxic secretions that ooze out of the toad's warts.

PLATE 12

Top left: This harlequin poison frog is just one of many species in the family Dendrobatidae that advertise their poisonous nature with bright warning colors. Poison frogs range from yellow, orange, and red to green, blue, and purple. Most have contrasting patterns of stripes, spots, or both. Some poison frogs are only mildly toxic. Others are toxic enough to kill a person if that person were stupid enough to eat it.

Top right: Green and black Oriental firebelly toads have poison glands in their skin. When threatened by a predator, the frog arches its back and raises his feet. This exposes its red-orange underside and warns the predator that the frog is poisonous. This behavior is called the unken reflex.

Bottom: Warty newts from Asia also have poison glands in their skin and exhibit the unken reflex when threatened by a predator. Their undersides are red, as you can see in this individual resting on a mirror.

PLATE 13

Brady Barr, host of National Geographic's "Dangerous Encounters" show, holds a Japanese giant salamander. How can he hold onto the 4-foot 9-inch, slippery creature!

PLATE 14

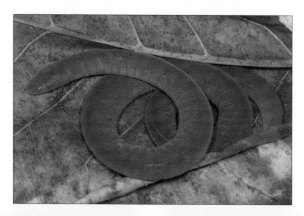

Top: This aquatic caecilian lives in slow-moving streams and rivers in South America. The back part of the body is laterally compressed, and the animal has no tail.

Middle left: A pink caecilian! This terrestrial caecilian, Boulenger's caecilian, is from Africa. These caecilians burrow underground. They have no tails.

Middle right: Asian tailed caecilians are widespread in Southeast Asia. These caecilians burrow into moist soil and leaf litter in rain forest and agricultural areas. They grow to nearly 20 inches in length.

Bottom: Pastaza River caecilians live in Colombia, Ecuador, and Peru. These caecilians belong to the same family as Boulenger's caecilians, and like them, they lack tails. Pastaza River caecilians live in both lowland forest and in human-disturbed areas such as gardens and plantations.

PLATE 15

Top: Florida worm lizards have long, thin bodies and no legs. They spend most of their lives underground where they eat termites, insect larvae, spiders, and other invertebrates. These lizards cannot see.

Bottom: In contrast, here's a reptile with eyes to die for! Fortunately for them, because smooth-fronted caiman are relatively small, they are less sought-after for their skins than are their larger crocodilian relatives.

PLATE 16

Top left: The rings of eastern coral snakes completely encircle the body, with the red and yellow rings touching each other. A popular ditty for distinguishing venomous coral snakes from their non-venomous mimics goes: "Red on yellow kill a fellow, red on black venom lack." The ditty doesn't work, as there are exceptions. The eastern coral snake, however, is one species that fits the ditty.

Top right: Some eastern diamondback rattlesnakes grow to over 80 inches in length. These large rattlesnakes make unnerving, loud buzzing sounds by shaking their rattles. The first time you hear a rattlesnake's warning, even if you don't see the snake, you know what it is!

Bottom: When threatened, a Cape cobra from southern Africa rears up, spreads its hood, and hisses. If that display doesn't frighten off the predator, the cobra might strike. This cobra's venom is the most potent of all the African cobras. If a human victim does not receive medical attention, he or she is likely to die within a few hours.

Herpetologists fear that soon many species of turtles from Southeast Asia will be gone forever.

In China, the Cantonese commonly eat snake meat. Specialties include soup made from five kinds of snakes, deep-fried snake meatballs, and fried shredded snake with vegetables. "Tiger Fights Dragon" is a popular dish — a combination of cat meat and snake meat. Lest you think that snake meat is a peculiarity eaten only by the Chinese, consider the following rattlesnake dishes eaten in the United States: rattlesnake casserole, stir-fried rattlesnake with grated coconut, fried rattlesnake marinated in orange and lemon juice with spices, barbequed rattlesnake, and baked rattlesnake smothered with cream of mushroom sauce.

A little over a decade ago, people killed large numbers of water snakes in Cambodia because the fish harvest wasn't as plentiful as usual. During the peak of the 1999–2000 wet season, Cambodians harvested and sold an average of 8500 water snakes every day. People ate the snake meat as an inexpensive substitute for fish. They also fed the snakes to crocodiles they were raising for sale. That was probably the largest harvest of any snake species in the world.

Pets

Amphibians and reptiles are popular as pets, especially bizarre, exotic, and brilliantly-colored species. Just within the United States, over 8 million amphibians and reptiles are currently kept as pets. Some popular ones include large-mouthed pac-man frogs; purple, blue, red, green, or yellow poison frogs;

big-eyed geckos; colorful chameleons; *arboreal* green iguanas; forked-tongued monitors; massive boas and pythons; and docile tortoises (Figure 77).

International trade of live amphibians and reptiles for pets is a big business, and it's growing. For example, in 1998 over 65,000 live reptiles were exported from Tanzania — mostly spinytailed lizards, geckos, and chameleons destined for the pet market. This is about 10 times as many live reptiles as the country exported in 1991. Following are examples of the numbers of animals that were collected from the wild worldwide during 1990–1994 to be sold as pets. And these are just the numbers we know about. In addition, there's a huge black market trade supplied by smugglers.

Figure 77. Spotted tree monitors, native to northern Australia and southern New Guinea, are kept as pets by herp enthusiasts.

Figure 78. It's much better to buy a captive-bred green iguana than to buy one captured from the wild. Wild iguanas belong in the wild.

- tortoises   214,924
- monitor lizards   228,091
- chameleons   278,413
- boas and pythons   652,124
- poison frogs   20,962

The United States is the world's largest buyer and seller of live reptiles. Approximately 2 million live reptiles have been imported into the country each year since the late 1990s. Nearly half of these are green iguanas (Figure 78). Fortunately, most of these iguanas are born in captivity, rather than caught in the wild. Each year, the United States exports more than 8 million red-eared slider turtles, born in captivity. These turtles are the world's most commonly sold and bought live reptile species.

The pet trade has two sides. On the one hand, more people interested in amphibians and reptiles means that more people will help conserve these animals and protect their habitats. On the other hand, each year many hundreds of thousands of amphibians and reptiles are collected in foreign countries and shipped to pet stores. Many of these die before they reach their destination. Those that do arrive alive rarely survive even six months in captivity because their new owners don't know how to care for their pets.

Folk and Modern Medicine

An estimated 80% of the world's people use folk medicines as their primary source of remedies. Amphibians and reptiles are among the most frequently used animals for these folk medicines. People use these medicines in the hope of curing rheumatism, heart disease, kidney problems, ulcers, cancer, and other ailments.

At least 165 species of reptiles are used in making traditional folk medicines worldwide. Of these, 53% are considered to be *endangered* species. A given reptile species is often used to treat multiple problems. For example, Mexicans swallow capsules containing the powder from dried rattlesnake skin, flesh, and ground-up bone to cure cancer, sores, rashes, pimples and acne, welts, itching, stress, heart disease, kidney disease, diabetes, and rheumatism. Because of the high demand for rattlesnake remedies, *population* sizes of these snakes have declined in Mexico.

Some species of turtles and snakes from southeast Asia are declining because of the high demand for their bodies or body parts. "Turtle jelly" is a black, gooey substance made from the *carapace* and *plastron* of the endangered golden coin turtle. The shell is boiled with medicinal herbs, including honeysuckle and chrysanthemum flowers. When eaten, it is believed to eliminate pimples and cure cancer and kidney failure. *Gui ban* is made from plastrons of Chinese softshell turtles. The plastrons are removed from the turtles, cleaned, dried in the sun, and then ground. Powders or pills of *gui ban* are believed to strengthen bones, reduce fever, calm the heart, reduce anxiety, and end sleeplessness. Taiwan currently imports over a hundred tons of turtle shells per year to make traditional medicines.

The Chinese add snakes to drinks in the belief that the snakes offer medicinal benefits. Snake gallbladder added to wine is believed to protect against sickness, and the person takes on the snake's strength. The medicinal drink *Wu Shiu Jiu* (five-snake wine) is believed to strengthen the body and help with joint ailments. The drink is made by soaking five kinds of venomous snakes in a large jar of distilled rice wine.

Many people believe that reptile fat has medicinal properties. In Asia, people smear fat from monitor lizards onto bacterial skin infections (Figure 79). Central Americans use fat from iguanas to heal burns and cuts. Crocodilian fat is used to cure asthma in the Dominican Republic and Haiti. Caiman fat is used in Brazil to treat rheumatism. In Madagascar, people treat burns and skin ulcers with crocodilian fat.

West Africans make traditional medicines from sea turtles. Fat from leatherbacks is used to treat convulsions, malaria, and liver problems, cure muscle sprains and bone fractures,

Figure 79. Many people consider the fat from common water monitors to have medicinal value.

and heal mouth wounds. Powdered sea turtle skulls and bones are used to reduce body aches. Mixed with honey or lemon juice, crushed sea turtle carapace is believed to cure headaches and asthma. The cooked heart or liver of green turtles is considered a cure for heart disease. Drinking the fresh blood of green turtles is used to relieve asthma. All sea turtles are endangered. Killing of these animals for traditional medicines no doubt affects their populations.

Not only cultures outside the United States use amphibians and reptiles in folk medicine. Some old remedies used within the United States include:

- To cure a toothache, roast 100 frogs in the oven. Make a powder of the dried bodies and then mix the powder with salt. Rub the mixture on your gums.

Figure 80. Do you think that toad pee would erase a wart?

- To get rid of a wart, let a toad pee on it. Then kill the toad (Figure 80).

- To stop bleeding, put a pile of frog eggs on the wound and let the eggs dry (Figure 81).

- To heal an open sore, fry a frog in fat. Cover the sore with the liquid from the pan.

- To get rid of a wart, cut off the head of a turtle and put some of the blood on the wart.

- To get rid of rheumatic pain, rub alligator fat onto the sore areas.

- To protect yourself from harm, wear a string of rattlesnake vertebrae around your neck.

- To cure and prevent headache, wear a rattlesnake's rattles in the lining of your hat.

People from many different cultures use secretions from toads as medicines. When a toad is disturbed, it may defend itself by secreting a white fluid from large *parotoid* glands on its head. This secretion tastes bad to a would-be predator and

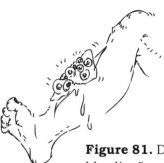

Figure 81. Do you think that frog eggs would stop a wound from bleeding?

may be irritating or poisonous as well. Eighteenth-century physicians used powder made from dried toads to lower a person's fever. The Chinese make a powder from toad secretions. Called *Ch'an Su*, the powder is mixed with flour and other ingredients and formed into cakes. *Ch'an Su* is used in treating heart ailments, for drying boils and abscesses, and for healing ulcers. Indian healers in Veracruz, Mexico, make medicines from toad secretions that also function as "love magic." It seems odd that toad secretions are so widely used as medicine, but it turns out they contain chemicals known to stimulate the human heart and to help the human body deal with stress.

Chinese giant salamanders have been used in traditional Chinese medicines for at least the past 2300 years. They are used in treating malaria, heavy-metal poisoning, Alzheimer's disease, and cancer. The salamanders are also used to make health and beauty products.

Amphibians and reptiles are used in modern medicine also. If you ever get bitten by a *venomous* snake, you may be rushed to the hospital to get a shot of *antivenin*, a substance that counteracts the snake's venom. Antivenin is made in a series of stages. First, venom is extracted from venomous snakes. Next, the venom is injected into a horse or sheep over and over, but not so much that it kills the animal. Eventually, the horse or sheep develops immunity to the venom. At this point the animal's blood contains antibodies, special proteins that destroy the venom. Blood is then drawn from the horse or sheep, and the serum containing the antibodies is purified in a laboratory. When this serum is injected into someone who has been bitten by a venomous snake, the person has a good chance of surviving — thanks to the antibodies produced by the horse or sheep. Venom extraction facilities around the world produce antivenins to save people's lives from snakebite.

Because frogs live in wet environments, they are constantly exposed to bacteria and fungi. Some species of frogs have chemicals in their mucous secretions that protect them from infection. An antibiotic cream has been made that contains a synthetic (man-made) form of certain chemicals found in the skin secretions of African clawed frogs (Figure 82). The cream is used to treat skin ulcers in people who have diabetes.

Research and Teaching

Amphibians and reptiles themselves, not just their chemicals, are in great demand for medical and biological research. We even send frog eggs to outer space to learn about the effects of weightlessness on development. Amphibians and reptiles are also widely used in teaching, for dissections and

Figure 82. African clawed frogs live in stagnant water often full of fungi, bacteria, and other microorganisms. They can live in these germy environments because their skin contains chemicals that function as antibiotics, antifungal, and antiparasitic agents.

demonstrations. Museums worldwide house millions of amphibian and reptile specimens pickled in formalin or alcohol (Figure 83).

Researchers and teachers generally buy amphibians and reptiles from biological supply houses, which buy the animals from people who make a living by collecting them in the wild. Unfortunately, most collectors are not concerned about the future of wild populations. They're out to make a profit, and they wipe out populations by capturing every animal possible. Then the collectors must move elsewhere.

In the early 1970s, most of the 13 million leopard frogs used in teaching and the additional 2 million leopard frogs used for research were captured from wild populations (Figure 84). One commercial supplier collected an average of 30 tons of frogs (about 1 million individuals) per year in the late 1960s.

Figure 83. Scientists collect and preserve specimens as part of their research, from anatomy to ecology.

Figure 84. Leopard frogs have long been used for educational purposes, such as dissection, and for medical and other research.

By 1973, the same supplier collected only 5 tons of frogs. The decrease wasn't because of lower demand. It was because field personnel couldn't find more frogs.

Humans affect amphibians and reptiles in other ways as well . . .

10
We Kill Them Indirectly, Too

Amphibians and reptiles suffer from humans in ways other than being collected as pets or killed for food, handbags, medicines, research, and education. Our activities often affect these animals even if we have no intention of harming them.

We modify or destroy their habitat. Animals that we introduce into areas where they don't occur naturally sometimes eat local amphibians and reptiles, destroy the habitat, or compete for food. We contaminate the environment with toxic chemicals that kill amphibians and reptiles.

Habitat Modification and Destruction

Ecologists and *conservation* biologists agree that the most fundamental threat to the environment is the growing human *population*. Our worldwide population in 2011 is nearly 7 billion. It's expected to reach 9.3 billion by the year 2050. This means an average increase of nearly 64 million more people in the world per year. The more people there are, the greater demand there is on the land (Figure 85). Each year humans need more land to support the extra people who weren't here the year before. More and more forests and open spaces that used to be home for amphibians and reptiles are being destroyed

Figure 85. The more people there are in the world, the greater the demand for oil. In 1967, Texaco discovered oil in the rain forest of eastern Ecuador. Texaco constructed a pipeline to get the oil out of the rain forest, over the Andes Mountains, and to the coast where it could be shipped out of the country. They also made a road all along the pipeline. Colonists flooded into the now-accessible area. This part of the Amazon Basin has been changed forever.

and converted to crop fields, shopping malls, and residential areas — places for humans to raise food, buy and sell goods, and live.

During the 1990s, about 80 acres of forest around the world were cut down every minute. That amounts to about 45 million acres every year — as much area as the states of Florida and Maryland combined. That's a lot of forest destroyed every year!

Only between 2% and 5% of original, uncut forest remains in the United States. The rest has been logged or disturbed in some way by humans. We cut down forests and convert the land to fields of corn, potatoes, wheat, or other crops. We used to leave wetlands (swamps and other wet areas) for frogs, salamanders, turtles, water snakes, and alligators because we thought these areas were unsuitable for humans. Now we drain the water, fill the areas with sand, and transform them into golf courses and shopping malls. Over the past 200 years, an estimated 120 million acres of wetlands in the United States have disappeared. Only recently have we realized that wetlands are not wastelands. They're a critical part of the landscape for wildlife.

The most extensive *deforestation* (clearing away of forests) is currently happening in the tropics. Scientists estimate that tropical rain forests currently cover less than 6% of Earth's surface but provide homes to over 50% of the known *species* of plants and animals. Over 80% of all amphibian and reptile species live in the tropics. More than half of the area originally covered in rain forest has already been cut down.

It's hard to estimate how much tropical forest is destroyed each year, but conservative estimates suggest about 32,256,000 acres. This figure of over 32 million is equivalent to the destruction of 29 city blocks of tropical forest per minute! Try to imagine an area of 29 city blocks in your city or town. Imagine this amount of tropical forest being cut down every minute!

At the current rate of deforestation, within 30 to 50 years most tropical forests will be gone. Haiti has already lost 99% of its original tropical forest. The Philippine Islands have lost 97%, and the island of Sri Lanka has lost more than 95%. Madagascar, home to 60% of the world's species of chameleons, has already lost 84% of its tropical forest.

Some tropical deforestation occurs because people need firewood, wood to build their homes, and land for farming (Figure 86). Sadly, however, much tropical deforestation is caused by human greed. We want more, and we want better. Tropical forests are cut down so that people can use exotic woods to make furniture. Huge areas of forest are converted to pasture for cattle that provide meat for the hamburgers we buy in fast-food restaurants. Wherever precious minerals are found,

Figure 86. The people who cleared land for their house in this Ecuadorian rain forest caused less damage than did the road crew that built a road nearby. Unfortunately, the two often go hand in hand.

the forest is destroyed so the minerals can be extracted from the earth. Roads are carved into the forest so the minerals can be trucked out.

The first thing most settlers do when they move to the rain forest is cut down the forest and burn the undergrowth vegetation to clear their land, a process called slash-and-burn agriculture. Then they plant crops. Most tropical soils are not very fertile. After two or three years the nutrients in the soil are used up or rain has washed them away. Another problem is that when some tropical soils are exposed to direct sunlight, they harden and can't retain moisture. So, the farmers cut down more forest and clear more land for their crops. Just think of all the animals that lose their homes in the process!

Eucalyptus trees, native to Australia, have been introduced to Africa, South America, Israel, Portugal, California, and other areas of the world (Figure 87). Why? Because the trees grow quickly, they are valuable sources of income. Their wood is used for timber, firewood, pulpwood, fence posts, and charcoal. The trees are also planted to serve as windbreaks and to reduce soil erosion. One problem is that native forest is cut down and replaced with the eucalyptus. Another problem is that these trees draw huge quantities of water from the soil.

Sometimes we destroy amphibian breeding sites just by modifying the environment, rather than by outright cutting down the forest. Most of us dislike mosquitoes, so we eliminate standing water where these insects lay their eggs. We replace drainage ditches with underground drainage systems. When we do this, mosquitoes aren't the only animals that lose their

Figure 87. In Chile, native forest was cut down and replanted in non-native eucalyptus trees.

breeding sites. Amphibians lose egg-laying sites also. The same thing happens when farmers and ranchers fill in their cattle-watering ponds and replace them with concrete or aluminum tanks, which are more efficient and convenient. Some treefrogs can scale the tank edges and lay their eggs in the water, but other frogs and salamanders are out of luck.

Introduction of Exotic Species

When humans settle a new place we often take along our domesticated animals: pigs, cattle, sheep, and goats for food, and dogs and cats for companionship. Rats get introduced into new areas accidentally. These exotic, or alien, animals can severely affect native populations of amphibians and reptiles, especially on islands. In some cases the aliens eat amphibians and reptiles or their eggs. In other cases they trample the habitat or compete with native amphibians and reptiles for food. Because these introduced animals don't have natural predators in their new environment, they often multiply quickly.

Tortoises on the Galápagos Islands in the Pacific have suffered not only from the sailors who ate them but also from introduced animals. Rats, who came as stowaways on explorers' ships, greedily devour tortoise eggs and hatchlings. Goats, intentionally introduced onto the islands, compete with tortoises for food. Dogs and cats eat young tortoises. Introduced pigs destroy the habitat while rooting and snuffling in search of food.

Tuatara have disappeared from the two large islands and some of the smaller islands of New Zealand. Again, the causes are likely competition and predation from sheep, goats, and rats introduced by early settlers.

In the 1870s, rats were such a problem in the sugarcane fields of Jamaica that mongooses were introduced from India to kill the rats. Mongooses don't eat only rats, however, and they don't stay in cane fields. They also feast on birds and reptiles — in or outside cane fields. Mongooses wiped out or drastically reduced populations of several species of lizards and one species of snake in Jamaica.

Introduced amphibians and reptiles themselves can be a menace. A good example is the brown tree snake which was unintentionally introduced onto the island of Guam, a territory of the United States, located about halfway between Japan and New Guinea. The snake probably arrived hidden in cargo, about 50 years ago. Brown tree snakes have reproduced so successfully on Guam that in some places there are now as many as 50 brown tree snakes in an area the size of a football field. Over time, the snake invaders have drastically reduced the populations of many species of birds and extinguished at least seven. Once birds became scarce, the snakes switched to lizards. Now they've greatly reduced or wiped out several lizard species as well.

Bullfrogs were introduced west of the Rocky Mountains beginning in the 1800s for human food. These large frogs have voracious appetites. In places where bullfrogs have been introduced, many of the native species of frogs have disappeared. People in many places of the world have tried to raise bullfrogs on "farms." Inevitably some escape. Once free, they devour the local amphibians.

Cuban tree frogs appeared in the lower Florida Keys in the 1800s, probably introduced by people (Figure 88). The frogs dispersed northward through the Everglades, and they kept marching north. Now isolated populations of this tree frog live in north Florida. Cuban tree frogs are good colonizers. They lay many eggs, can tolerate a wide range of environmental conditions, have few predators, and consume a diverse diet. Included in their diverse diet are native frogs.

Aquatic invaders have caused the decline or disappearance of amphibians. Trout have been introduced into many

Figure 88. One reason that Cuban tree frogs are such good colonizers is that they eat a wide variety of food. In Florida, they eat native green tree frogs, squirrel tree frogs, leopard frogs, southern toads, and eastern narrow-mouth toads.

rivers and lakes worldwide, both as a source of food and for recreation. Because trout love to eat tadpoles, stream- or lake-breeding frogs decline in areas where trout have been introduced. Tiny mosquitofish, introduced into many areas to control mosquitoes, don't eat only mosquito larvae. They also eat salamander larvae and tadpoles. Fishermen often buy live crayfish as bait and then dump the leftovers into the lake or stream. These newcomers often thrive and breed — and eat amphibian eggs and larvae.

Another problem is that alien species such as bullfrogs, fish, and crayfish often carry parasites. Local amphibians can then be infected with these parasites or catch diseases from these aliens.

Environmental Pollution

Humans also affect amphibians and reptiles by polluting the air, water, and soil (Figure 89). Gasoline and oil wash off

Figure 89. This oil spill in eastern Ecuador has destroyed a frog breeding pond.

roads and seep into the ground nearby. Pesticides and fertilizers wash into areas where amphibians and reptiles live. Chemicals from mining and logging operations and from industrial plants poison the land and water. Some pollutants are carried long distances from one country to another, in the air or water. For example, contaminants blow over from Africa to the Caribbean region, Central America, and northern South America. Pollutants can kill amphibians and reptiles, stunt their growth, or affect reproduction.

Two chemicals released in automobile exhaust and by coal-burning factories, nitrogen oxide and sulfur dioxide, harm amphibians. Wind spreads these chemicals over wide areas.

Mixed with water in the atmosphere, the chemicals turn to nitric acid and sulfuric acid. Falling rain picks up these chemicals and becomes *acid rain*. Many amphibians can't tolerate acid conditions in water where they breed. Their eggs and larvae die, or they develop abnormally. Declines of some populations of natterjack toads from Britain may be due to acid rain.

In 1995, schoolchildren on a fieldtrip found many abnormal leopard frogs around a farm pond in Minnesota. These frogs had missing legs, twisted legs, stubby legs, extra legs, or double feet. Some frogs were missing an eye. People have found large numbers of abnormal leopard frogs and other species of frogs elsewhere in the United States and in Canada within the past decade (Figure 90). What's causing the abnormalities?

People worried that something in the Minnesota pond water might be affecting development of the eggs or tadpoles. The water might be contaminated by pesticides, excess nitrogen from fertilizers, or poisonous heavy metals such as mercury and lead. Would people be affected also? Public health officials tested water from the Minnesota pond. They found no toxic chemicals. In some places in the world, though, toxic chemicals are responsible for amphibian developmental abnormalities.

Parasitic flatworms called trematodes likely caused the abnormalities found in the Minnesota leopard frogs. The *life cycle* of these tiny parasites, hardly longer than a pinhead, involves birds, snails, and amphibians. As adults, the trematodes live in the digestive tract of birds. When an infected bird defecates in a pond, the trematode eggs from the bird's feces

Figure 90. This 5-legged juvenile bullfrog is unlikely to survive to maturity. It will be easy prey for a snake, bird, or other predator.

hatch. The young trematodes infect pond snails. In time, the trematodes reproduce inside the snails. This time, a different trematode body form hatches from the eggs. The young lodge in tadpoles, near the site of developing hind limbs. Their presence disrupts normal limb development and results in *metamorphosed* frogs without legs or with extra legs. Birds eat the abnormal, trematode-infected frogs, and the cycle begins again.

Some chemical pollutants interfere with animals' hormone systems. Hormones are molecules produced by glands, released into the blood, and transported throughout the body. They serve as a chemical messenger system, and they influence various body functions. Medical researchers and biologists think that the hormone systems of many animals, including amphibians and reptiles, are being disrupted by chemical contamination in the environment.

One particularly nasty group of synthetic, toxic compounds are polychlorinated biphenyls (PCBs for short). PCBs were once widely used in plastics, paints, and adhesives. In 1979, the United States government prohibited further production of PCBs and banned their use. Medical research suggested that exposure to large amounts of PCBs was associated with birth defects, liver damage, and cancer in people. PCBs also cause reproductive failure in fishes, birds, and mammals. Unfortunately, PCBs stay in the environment a long time and are transported long distances through the air. Traces of PCBs are still found in air, soil, ocean water, and animal tissues in the United States, even though they haven't been used for more than 20 years.

Some PCB compounds are so similar to estrogen (a hormone that affects female characteristics and behavior) that they act like estrogen when they get into an animal's body. One study of red-eared slider turtles showed that PCBs can change the sex of embryos that are developing into males (Figure 91). Instead of males, the embryos develop into females.

Lake Apopka in central Florida has been contaminated with chemicals due to a major spill from a nearby pesticide plant. These chemicals have had harmful effects on reproductive success of the resident alligators. Many embryos die before they hatch, and hormone levels in both males and females are abnormal.

141

Figure 91. If, in a given population, only female red-eared sliders are produced because of PCBs in the environment, eventually the population will go extinct.

One of the major reasons we can produce so much food is that we spray our crops with pesticides to get rid of weeds, insects, and fungus. Scientists have shown recently that atrazine, one of the world's most widely-used weed-killers, causes abnormalities in amphibians. Some individuals exposed to atrazine develop both male and female reproductive organs. When this happens, the animals can function as neither sex. In one species tested, males exposed to atrazine developed smaller than normal larynges, the organs male frogs use to call and attract female frogs. If males can't call normally, they can't mate.

Another type of pollution is solid waste. Think about the amount of garbage your family produces every week. Where does it go? Some of it might be recycled. Much gets buried in the ground, in landfills. Until 1992, the United States dumped millions of tons of waste, including chemicals, household trash, human waste from sewerage systems, plastics, and industrial waste, into the oceans each year. We thought it didn't do any harm in the oceans because we assumed the oceans were large enough to absorb it. The marine animals have to live (or die) with it, though. Since 1992 it has been illegal to dump waste into the ocean. Some of the trash that's already there will last a long time. A tin can will last 50 years, and an aluminum Coke can will last 200 years in the ocean.

An estimated 24,000 tons of plastic used to be dumped into the oceans each year. Leatherback sea turtles eat mainly jellyfish, and a floating plastic bag resembles a jellyfish. In some areas, half the leatherbacks examined have plastic garbage in their intestines. The plastic probably interferes with the turtles' ability to digest food and to breathe. Some plastics are toxic and may be slowly poisoning the turtles. Plastics will litter the ocean for a long time because they break down slowly. Disposable diapers and plastic bottles will last about 450 years in the ocean.

Our trash kills amphibians and reptiles on land also. The animals get stuck in discarded plastic holders that keep 6-packs of cans together. They get tied up in twine, rope, and wire. And they get trapped in pieces of plastic netting that people use to control erosion and to protect their fruit crops from hungry birds (Figure 92).

Figure 92. Plastic netting can trap and ensnare wildlife, such as this unfortunate whipsnake.

Global warming is also affecting amphibians and reptiles . . .

11
Who Turned Up the Heat?

For nearly 40 years, climatologists (scientists who study Earth's weather conditions) have warned that temperatures across the planet are getting warmer. We're living in times of "global warming." Over the past century, temperatures worldwide have risen nearly 2 degrees Fahrenheit. Climatologists predict that within the next 10 years, average temperatures will be warmer than at any other time during the past 1000 years. Predictions of temperature increases are based on computer models. A "best guess" estimate is an increase above 1980–1990 temperatures of 3.2 to 7.2 °F by the end of the 21st century.

Warmer temperatures will change the land area of deserts, wetlands, and forests. In some places these environments will expand. In others they will shrink in size. If ice melts in the Arctic and Antarctic, sea levels will rise and flood coastal habitats such as mangrove swamps.

Humans cause much of this warming trend. We release huge amounts of heat-trapping gases, especially carbon dioxide, into the atmosphere. Carbon dioxide is released when we burn oil, coal, and natural gas. Trees and other plants absorb carbon dioxide. When we cut down forests, there are fewer plants to absorb the gas, and carbon dioxide in Earth's

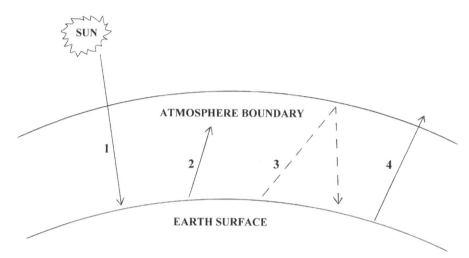

Figure 93. In the greenhouse effect: (1) Incoming heat energy from the sun warms Earth's surface, (2) The warmed surface radiates heat energy toward space, (3) Greenhouse gases trap and reradiate heat energy back toward Earth, keeping the surface warm, and (4) Limited amounts of heat escape from Earth's atmosphere.

atmosphere increases. Carbon dioxide traps heat, so with more of this gas in Earth's atmosphere, less heat can escape into space. This process is called the "greenhouse effect" because Earth's atmosphere traps heat much like the glass or plastic walls and roof of a greenhouse (Figure 93).

Along with warmer temperatures, climatologists predict that: (1) soils will become drier; (2) dry seasons will last longer; (3) the amount of rainfall will vary more from year to year; and (4) some areas will get more rain than normal, others areas will get less rain than normal. Global warming and drier — or more variable — conditions will probably occur gradually over our lifetimes.

Amphibians will be greatly affected by global warming. Recall that their skin loses water easily and must be kept moist for the mucous glands to function efficiently. Amphibians stress easily when exposed to warm temperatures.

Can reptiles outrun global warming? Most reptiles don't stress readily from warm temperatures; they are good at resisting water loss thanks to their dry skin and scales; and they can tolerate high body temperatures. Nonetheless, they aren't immune to global warming.

In the short-term picture, amphibians and reptiles can respond to warmer, drier conditions in three ways. They can move into more suitable habitats. They can stay where they are and adapt to the changing conditions. Or they can die.

Few amphibians and reptiles can follow the first option. Some small salamanders and lizards don't roam more than 10 feet from the center of their *home range* (the area within which an animal moves about in its daily activities) within their lifetimes. These animals almost certainly won't be able to move into better habitat. Frogs that normally travel a mile or more in search of breeding ponds may be better able to move, but only if they don't encounter barriers, such as dry fields. In general, snakes and turtles move around more than do lizards and amphibians. Some big turtles and snakes have home ranges larger than 50 acres (the area of about 40 football fields). In theory, animals that travel far in search of food could migrate in search of better habitat. But we're changing the landscape. They too will encounter barriers such as roads and cities that prevent them from reaching cooler or wetter places.

Adaptability is the ability to adjust to changes. Not all amphibians and reptiles are equally *adaptable*. Garter snakes are very adaptable (Figure 94). They can live in many different habitats, including city parks and around people's homes, because they tolerate a wide range of temperatures and eat a wide variety of prey. If the average temperature this year is half a degree warmer than last year, it's no big deal for them. If fewer frogs are out and about because the climate is drier, garter snakes will eat grasshoppers instead. The more adaptable a *species* is, the more likely it is to survive global warming.

Some amphibians and reptiles are *specialized*. That is, they can survive only within a narrow set of conditions. They

Figure 94. Garter snakes eat just about any animal they can overpower and get into their mouths, from slugs and earthworms to baby birds and rodents.

may tolerate only a certain range of temperature and humidity, or perhaps they eat only ants. Specialized species have a hard time coping with environmental change, such as warmer, drier conditions.

There isn't much to say about the third option: death. Species that can't or don't move elsewhere may die if they can't adapt to climatic changes.

In the long-term picture, if climate changes happen gradually, over many generations of a given species, some *populations* may adapt to the changes. Individuals that make up a given population vary in their genetic make-up, including traits that relate to the ability to tolerate environmental conditions. If the climate becomes warmer and drier, individuals that can best tolerate the changed conditions will be most likely to survive and reproduce or produce the most offspring. Their genetic traits for ability to tolerate the climatic conditions will be passed on to their offspring. With time, the population will become better adapted to the warmer, drier environment. *Evolution* — change in the genetic makeup of the population over time — will have occurred.

Warmer, drier conditions might affect amphibians and reptiles in many ways. Here are some possibilities and some questions to ponder:

- There might be less food for species that eat small insects. Many small insects can't survive dry conditions, so they'll die. Other insects might hide out in cooler, wetter places where they're hard to find. What will insect-eating amphibians and reptiles find to eat?

- Activity patterns might change. Some species might be active more hours each day and more days each year. Other species might be less active because they can't tolerate the warmer temperatures. How will interactions among species change?

- Warmer, drier conditions might stress amphibians and reptiles and depress their immune systems. Will they become more vulnerable to diseases?

- With less rain, ponds would hold water for less time. When there is water, all the frogs might come to lay eggs at once. The result would be hundreds of thousands of tadpoles in a pond. Will there be enough food for them to develop into froglets?

- Amphibians that lay their eggs on land might have trouble finding moist sites. Once they find them, will the sites dry up before the eggs hatch? Reptile eggs might die also if the air is too dry.

- Warmer temperatures might change the numbers of males versus females that are born. As mentioned earlier, the incubation temperature of some reptile eggs determines whether the hatchlings will be male or female (Figure 95). In general, warmer temperatures cause turtle and crocodilian embryos to become female. Colder temperatures cause them to become male. In some species of lizards where gender depends on incubation temperature, warmer temperatures cause embryos to become male, but in other species warmer temperatures cause embryos to become female. How would birth of all males or all females affect the future of these species?

Figure 95. These leatherback sea turtles have just hatched and are on their way to the ocean. Ideally, their nest temperature produced approximately half males and half females within the clutch.

Is there existing evidence that amphibians are affected by climate change? Yes, and the research so far suggests that different species respond to warmer temperatures in different ways. For example, investigators analyzed records gathered over a period of 100 years of the earliest calling dates for males of six species of frogs from Ithaca, New York. In cold climates such as Ithaca, male frogs don't begin to call until temperatures warm in the spring. The investigators found that by the end of the 20th century, four of the frog species called 10 to 13 days earlier than they had at the beginning of the 20th century. The other two species had not changed their activity periods. Likewise, a study in the United Kingdom revealed that while two frog species and one salamander species were breeding 1 to 3 weeks earlier per decade from 1978 to 1994, another frog species had not changed. In contrast, a study in Japan focused on one salamander species and two frog species over a period of 12 to 31 years. All populations exhibited a trend toward earlier breeding in recent years, associated with warmer temperatures earlier in the season.

What does earlier breeding mean for amphibians? There can be both good and bad consequences. If cold winter temperatures set in later in the year and spring temperatures warm earlier in the year, amphibians will have longer to reproduce. Species that normally deposit only one clutch of eggs per year might be able to lay an additional clutch. The down side is that several studies have revealed that many species of amphibians need to hibernate. If they don't, they don't grow as large and they don't produce as many eggs (Figure 96). This would reduce their potential reproductive success.

In the Andes Mountains of southern Peru, three species of frogs have colonized newly formed ponds in areas where glacier ice has melted due to warming temperatures. These frogs are now living in areas between 17,210 and 17,550 feet — the highest elevations of any frogs in the world. How many more frogs will migrate upward and colonize new ice-free, warmer areas? How will these range extensions affect local *ecosystems*? These are questions waiting to be answered.

Evidence also suggests that reptiles are already affected by climate change. In a study published in 2010, investigators compared recent and past surveys of 48 species of lizards at 200 sites in Mexico. They found that since 1975, 12% of the populations surveyed had gone extinct. The likelihood of

Figure 96. Clutch size (number of eggs laid) in most amphibians, including this spotted salamander, usually varies with body size. Larger females generally produce more eggs.

extinction was correlated with the amount of warming at a given site during the spring. The greater the temperature increase, the greater the likelihood of extinction. When temperatures get too warm, lizards spend more time in cooler refuges. If they spend less time foraging for food in the spring months, they store less energy for reproduction. Less reproduction leads to a greater likelihood of population extinction.

The scientists also reported that populations of lizards on five continents have gone extinct since 1975. Many of these lived in protected nature preserves. The investigators concluded that global warming was responsible. The scientists predicted that by the year 2080, lizard population extinctions will reach 39% worldwide. Extinctions of entire species of lizards may reach 20% by 2080.

Another change that might affect amphibians, and perhaps also reptiles, is an increase in the amount of UV (ultraviolet) radiation from the sun that now reaches Earth's surface. Ultraviolet rays are both good and bad for animals. They stimulate bone growth, but they also cause sunburn and encourage development of skin cancer. You smear sunscreen on yourself to shield your skin from UV rays. Amphibians have no sunscreen. Ultraviolet radiation can slowly cause blindness. You wear sunglasses to block out UV rays from your eyes (Figure 97). Exposure to high levels of UV rays can also damage

Figure 97. We can wear sunglasses to protect our eyes from UV radiation. Amphibians can't.

154

amphibians' eyes, and they can't put on sunglasses. Many amphibians lay their eggs in shallow water where the sun warms the water and allows the eggs to develop quickly. The negative part of being exposed to direct sunlight is that high doses of UV radiation can cause amphibian embryos to develop abnormally and even die. Amphibians predicted to suffer the most from increased UV radiation are those that live at high elevations in the mountains where the rays are much stronger than at lower elevations.

Sometimes the amount of UV radiation striking frog or salamander eggs isn't enough by itself to cause damage. Increased UV radiation, however, can make the eggs more vulnerable to fungus infection. Ultimately, the embryos die from the fungus. There might also be an interaction between UV radiation and acid rain. Either factor alone might not kill amphibian eggs, but the combination could be lethal.

Ultraviolet radiation is a bigger problem now than it was 30 years ago. Why? The *ozone* (a form of oxygen) layer in the upper atmosphere of Earth is becoming thinner each year. The ozone layer normally blocks out most UV radiation, serving as our global sunscreen. With a thinner ozone layer, more UV radiation comes through and strikes Earth's surface.

Chemicals called chlorofluorocarbons, CFCs for short, cause much of the thinning of the ozone layer. CFCs are compounds of chlorine, fluorine, and carbon. These compounds don't smell and you can't see them. They're used as cooling substances in refrigerators and air conditioners; in cleaning agents and plastic foams; and as propellants in aerosol spray cans. Every time someone sprays deodorant or insect repellent from an aerosol can containing these chemicals, CFCs are released into the air. About 35 years ago scientists discovered that CFCs float up into the ozone layer. There, UV rays strike these chemicals. The CFCs break apart and release chlorine. The atoms of chlorine react with ozone and change the ozone to ordinary oxygen, which doesn't have the UV-screening abilities of ozone.

Since the late 1970s, the United States, Canada, and many other countries have banned the use of CFCs in aerosol spray cans. Unfortunately, however, CFCs are still used in aerosol cans manufactured in other countries and are still used for other purposes as well. More than 100 nations are working together to reduce the amount of CFCs released into the air. Even if CFCs were completely banned today, we'd still have a problem: CFCs are hard to break down, and they float around in the air for a long time. Some scientists estimate that about 95% of the CFCs released since 1955 are still making their way up to destroy the ozone layer. Even if all CFCs were banned today, damage to our sunscreen layer might continue throughout the 21st century.

Amphibians also have to deal with the killer fungus . . .

12
Attack of the Killer Fungus!

"Marty, the golden toads are out! You've got to come see them!" Wolf Guindon, field coordinator for the Monteverde Cloud Forest Reserve in northern Costa Rica, shivered in the rain at my front door, urging me to join him for the annual spectacle.

I met up with Wolf the following day, in early April, 1987. We hiked uphill through a constant drizzle to the elfin forest. As we rounded a bend on the path we saw more than 100 brilliant golden-orange male toads gathered around small pools of water at the bases of stunted trees (Figure 98; Plate 1). The toads, sparkling like jewels on the dark ground, were waiting for females to emerge from underground. We soon found several pairs of toads laying eggs. Females were colored differently from males. Instead of uniform golden-orange, the females had black, yellow, and scarlet-red blotches.

Over the next 10 days, hundreds of golden toads laid eggs. Soon it stopped raining and the breeding pools dried. So did most eggs. May brought another heavy rainstorm and more golden toads laid eggs. Those pools also dried before many eggs hatched. During the breeding season, I had seen more than 1500 golden toads, but very few of their eggs had hatched.

I returned to Costa Rica the following April. The toads had disappeared, except for one lone male sitting next to a

Figure 98. These male golden toads have gathered around a pool of water at the base of a tree. They are waiting for females to emerge from underground to breed.

pool. I assumed that the weather was too dry and that the toads were hanging out in the moist underground. I returned the following year. That year, 1989, my graduate student Frank Hensley saw the last golden toad ever reported.

What happened to the toads? The forest reserve where the toads lived is protected from habitat disturbance and from collectors. The toads should have been safe. The year 1986–1987 was unusually warm and dry. Did the toads dry up and die? Sometimes when an amphibian *population* disappears, individuals from nearby populations colonize the area. In the case of golden toads, this was impossible. As far as we know, by 1987 only one population of golden toads existed, and that was the one I had studied. By 2011, 22 years after Frank found that last toad, no additional toads have been seen, despite researchers carrying out annual searches.

Golden toads are just one example of amphibians that have mysteriously disappeared without an obvious reason such as habitat destruction. Populations of boreal toads have declined or disappeared from the Rocky Mountains in Colorado. Eight *species* of frogs declined or disappeared from northeastern Queensland in Australia. Populations of many frogs declined or disappeared from Costa Rica and Panama in Central America (Figure 99). Ditto for Ecuador in South America and in many other areas of the world.

During the 1990s, investigators found dead frogs on the ground in Australia and in Central America. Examination of the bodies revealed presence of a *parasite* that turned out to be the fungus mentioned earlier in Chapter Six. This fungus,

Figure 99. Harlequin frogs are one of the many frog species from Costa Rica whose populations are declining and disappearing.

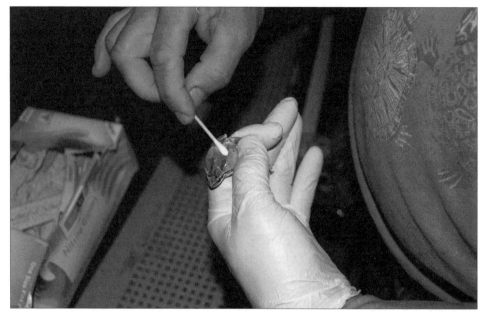

Figure 100. Using a glove to avoid contamination, a biologist rubs a cotton swab onto a frog's skin. The swab will be placed in a sterile vial and later analyzed for the presence of Bd.

Batrachochytrium dendrobatidis, or Bd for short, is the only member of the phylum Chytridiomycota that parasitizes *vertebrates*. And the only vertebrates it attacks are amphibians. Scientists named the fungus as a new genus and species in 1999.

Scientists now have found frogs attacked by Bd on all continents, except Antarctica where there are no amphibians (Figure 100). How did Bd end up in so many places? One possibility is that the fungus is a widespread organism that has only recently become deadly to amphibians. Perhaps amphibians have become more vulnerable to Bd because of environmental changes or stress. Or, perhaps Bd has become more deadly in recent years. An alternative hypothesis is that Bd is an exotic invader — an introduced organism that is spreading through areas. If so, amphibians previously unexposed to the fungus might be especially vulnerable to attack.

In addition to trying to figure out if Bd is a widespread, native organism or an exotic invader, scientists are addressing other questions. If Bd is an invader, how is it spread across widely separated geographical regions? Is there a link between climate change and vulnerability to Bd? Does stress increase likelihood of contracting the disease? Why are some amphibian species more susceptible to the fungus than are others?

Once Bd starts to kill amphibians in a given area, is there anything we can do to stop the fungus? All we can do is remove the amphibians. This has already been done in Panama. Scientists predicted that Bd would soon reach El Valle, a town and national park in the bowl of an inactive volcano. A team of employees and volunteers from Zoo Atlanta and the Atlanta Botanical Garden in Georgia traveled to El Valle in 2006 before Bd arrived at the site. They collected 600 individuals of 35 frog species and flew them back to Georgia. Many of the frogs are breeding successfully in captivity.

As predicted, Bd arrived in El Valle in spring 2006 and killed many of the remaining frogs. Many people consider the heroic airlift to have been worthwhile, but it brings up ethical questions. For how long and at what expense should scientists undertake such efforts? How do we choose which species to rescue? How do we choose which sites should receive our time, energy, and money?

Figure 101. Golden frogs are a Panamanian national symbol.

One amphibian rescued from El Valle is the endangered golden frog (not to be confused with the golden toad of Costa Rica; Figure 101). For many hundreds of years, people have considered these frogs sacred. One legend says that anyone fortunate enough to see one will have good luck and find happiness. Now the hope is that someday the habitat will become Bd-free, and the descendents of the golden frogs transported to Georgia can go home to Panama. If golden frogs and other species rescued from El Valle are zoo captives forever, was the airlift worth it?

Many *herpetologists* now suspect that Bd is responsible for many of the "mysterious" declines and local extinctions of frogs and salamanders worldwide. I wonder if Bd killed the golden toads from the Monteverde Cloud Forest Reserve.

∽

People will protect amphibians and reptiles only if they think these animals are worthy of protection. A relevant question, then, is how do people around the world feel about amphibians and reptiles?

13

Good or Bad? Love or Hate?

People's actions cause some amphibians and reptiles to decline and others to disappear. But people also can be part of the solution to the problem. How do we start? We begin by improving the way people feel about amphibians and reptiles.

Conservation organizations spend millions of dollars each year to protect pandas, whales, elephants, and gorillas. This is necessary, and it's good, but amphibians and reptiles are often ignored. Out of each dollar spent on conservation of wildlife, less than a nickel is spent on amphibians and reptiles. Why?

Attitudes toward amphibians and reptiles are mixed. Many people think these animals aren't worth worrying about. Others think amphibians and reptiles are ugly and boring, or they're afraid of them. The words "amphibians" and "reptiles" are even associated with bad people. One definition of reptile in my dictionary is "a groveling, sneaky, very mean person." A definition of toad is "a despicable person." Toads and snakes have other bad word associations. Have you heard the expression, "Ugly as a toad?" (Figure 102) Or "Mean as a snake?" To "toady" up to someone means to flatter to get into the person's good graces. A "snake in the grass" is someone who seems harmless but is actually evil or dangerous. The expression "lower than a snake's belly" refers to something mean or nasty.

Figure 102. Indeed, "Ugly as a toad . . ."

Worldwide, people have as many positive as negative atti-tudes toward amphibians and reptiles. Many people worship these animals. They respect them for various reasons and fight to protect them. Consider the following examples of attitudes that reflect "good or bad," "love or hate."

All over the world, from the past to the present, people associate frogs with rain. Indigenous Pre-Colombian artists from Central America crafted frogs from solid gold (Figure 103). They placed these frogs on hilltops or wore them as jewelry in the belief that the gold frogs would bring rain. In some parts of India and Bangladesh, villagers hold marriage ceremonies be-tween male and female frogs as rituals to the rain gods during droughts. A priest marries the frog couple in the belief that rain will follow, allowing the villagers to plant their crops. After

Figure 103. These replicates of the solid gold originals just might bring rain also!

the happy couple is blessed, the villagers release the frogs into a nearby pond.

Because frogs seem to appear from nowhere following a hard rain, people associate them with resurrection, rebirth, and renewal. One Egyptian legend tells that eight gods, four of which had frog heads, created the world. Egyptians dried frogs and buried them with their human dead. In China, amulets (charms) in the shapes of frogs carved from jade were placed on the tongues of deceased people and buried with them.

Ancient Egyptians worshipped frogs as a symbol of fertility. This made perfect sense, because many *species* of frogs lay thousands of eggs in one clutch. Egyptian women who wished to get pregnant wore gold frog-shaped amulets. Hekt, the Egyptian life-giving goddess, was represented as a woman with a frog's head. She represented fertility and presided over women as they gave birth. Ancient Egyptian women often wore amulets in the shape of Hekt to protect them during childbirth.

People throughout the world have long worn frog amulets for good luck. Romans believed that frogs brought good luck to a home. The Japanese word for frog, *kaeru*, also means "to return." Japanese often carry a small frog amulet when they travel, to ensure their safe return home. In many rural areas of the United States people believe that if newlyweds see a toad on the road, they will have a happy marriage. Abundant toads on your land are believed to be a sign of great harvest and increasing wealth (Figure 104).

Many people believe that frogs have supernatural powers, probably because of their "magical" *metamorphosis* from the tadpole stage into a 4-legged frog. Their croaking is believed

Figure 104. Great harvest and increasing wealth! Now that's worth encouraging toads on your land!

to bring rain, and frogs themselves are thought to have power to heal and cleanse. According to legends in both the Old and New worlds, lunar eclipses happen when a great frog swallows the moon. In Siberia, India, and China, legends teach that the world rests on a frog's back. Whenever the frog moves, earthquakes shake the world.

On the negative side, many people believe that toads cause warts. Toads often symbolize ugliness in literature and folktales. Shakespeare referred to the toad as "ugly and venomous." In his play *Richard III*, Shakespeare referred to the king as "a poisonous hunch-back'd toad." Frogs in early Christianity symbolized uncleanliness because they live in the mud. Folklore suggests that toads should be avoided because they are evil. One belief: a toad's breath will cause convulsions in children. Frogs are not presented in a very good way in the Bible. They are the second plague that God sent to Egypt with the demand to Pharaoh to let His people go. In medieval Europe, frogs and toads symbolized the devil because the Catholic church associated them with ingredients in witches' brews (Figure 105).

Ancient legend claims that salamanders were created from fire. There's a rational explanation for this belief. Salamanders often seek shelter inside damp logs lying on the ground. When people brought logs indoors and threw them onto their fires, sometimes salamanders crawled out. To this day, salamanders are associated with heat and fire. The word salamander is used for wood stoves, heaters, grills, and ovens.

Another belief was that salamanders could withstand any amount of heat. Perhaps this belief came about because when

Figure 105. As Shakespeare wrote in his play *Macbeth*, "Round about the cauldron go; In the poison'd entrails throw. Toad, that under cold stone, Days and nights hast thirty-one, Swelter'd venom sleeping got, Boil thou first i' the charmed pot. Double, double toil and trouble; Fire burn and cauldron bubble."

many salamanders become frightened or disturbed, they secrete a milky mucus. This mucus might protect the animal from heat for just a moment as it flees the fire. Salamanders were also thought to be able to put out fires. These assumed qualities lead people to believe that salamanders had supernatural and extraordinary powers.

Salamanders also are associated with evil. The witches in Shakespeare's play *Macbeth* use "eye of newt" as an ingredient in their magic potion. (Newts are a type of salamander; Figure 106.) During the Middle Ages in Europe, people were awarded gold coins for killing salamanders because these amphibians

Figure 106. Does this newt look evil?

were considered wicked. Also during the Middle Ages, in some places in eastern Europe, witches used brandy made from salamanders to conjure up demons. Irish country folk believed that if a person slept in a field with his or her mouth open, newts would enter the body and cause sickness. For this reason, people poisoned newts' water and caught and killed the salamanders.

In Roman mythology, because lizards slept through the winter, they symbolized death and subsequent resurrection. In ancient Greece and Egypt, lizards symbolized divine wisdom and good fortune. Perhaps this association came about because lizards can drop their tails to protect themselves — and then grow new ones.

Because chameleons can rapidly change their appearance, they have been and still are associated with people who change their appearance, thoughts, or words. We call a person who does this a "chameleon." In early Christianity the chameleon symbolized the devil, who took on different appearances to deceive people.

In some places horned lizards are considered to be good omens (Figure 107; Plate 8). People along the Texas-Mexico border believe the lizards bring much-needed rain. Children on the Navajo Nation in Arizona and New Mexico hold horned lizards to their hearts and murmur, "Yáat' ééh shi che," — "Hello my grandfather." As thanks for this respectful greeting, the lizards give the children strength. For thousands of years, continuing to the present, many Native American tribes in the southwestern United States believe that horned lizards have the power to bestow happiness and good health.

On the South Pacific island of New Caledonia, people don't kill lizards because they believe lizards might carry their own ancestors' souls. In contrast, Iranians often kill lizards because

Figure 107. If the person holding this horned lizard is respectful, will the lizard bestow good health and happiness?

171

they believe lizards carry the devil's soul. Some people from Thailand hate monitor lizards because they believe that monitors dig up graves and eat human flesh.

On Mindanao in the Philippine Islands, locals hesitate to live in thatched huts where there are no geckos. They figure that if geckos aren't there, something must be wrong with the place. In Thailand, many people think just the opposite. They don't want geckos in their homes because they believe geckos bring bad luck. Just think how differently people on Mindanao versus Thailand would feel if you tried to protect the local geckos. People on Mindanao would be glad to help. Thai people would be horrified.

Because of their strong shells, turtles seem well designed to carry burdens on their backs. Perhaps this explains the myths from India, China, Japan, and North and South America of huge turtles that support the mountains and even entire continents. People from these cultures respect turtles (Figure 108).

Many turtles, especially tortoises, live a long time. For this reason, turtles symbolize long life and immortality. Ancient Chinese often used turtle designs in burials. Some burial mounds were turtle-shaped. Turtles were embroidered on burial clothes. Huge, carved stone turtles supported the memorial tablets that marked the graves of emperors and other nobles. People all over the world still view turtles as symbols of longevity. At the Turtle Temple in Bangkok, Thailand, visitors feed captive turtles and pray for long lives.

People have used turtle amulets for a long time. Ancient Egyptians wore turtle-shaped amulets for protection and good

Figure 108. Who wouldn't love a box turtle?

health. In many Native American cultures of North America, the umbilical cord of a newborn baby is placed in an amulet bag, often in the shape of a turtle. The amulet is believed to protect the child and keep him or her connected both to Mother and to Mother Earth. The bag is attached to the baby's cradleboard or worn by the mother.

Tortoises and many other turtles have steady, deliberate movements. This characteristic suggests endurance and perseverance. In Celtic symbolism, the turtle teaches us to be grounded, in tune with Earth, and to "go with the flow." The fact that the turtle is self-contained, living within its home, suggests focus and self-reliance.

Not all cultures respect turtles. Ancient Egyptians associated turtles with the Underworld. Turtles symbolized darkness and evil, enemies of Ra, the Sun god. Legend had it that as Ra traveled through the Underworld "dangerous" creatures, including turtles, tried to attack the god. For the Aztecs, turtles symbolized cowardice and boastfulness because, although turtles are hard on the outside, they are soft inside. People in some parts of the Amazon Basin kill turtles because they believe them to be evil.

Ancient Egyptians considered crocodiles divine because they brought the rains that made the Nile overflow and fertilize the land. The people had a crocodile god named Sobek. They worshipped Sobek to appease him and to insure fertility of their crops. In the reptiles' honor, Egyptians built a city they named Sobek. The Greeks later renamed the holy city Crocodilopolis ("Crocodile City"). In parts of Madagascar, people worship crocodiles because they believe these reptiles possess the spirits of former chiefs. In Borneo, people protect crocodiles because they believe crocodiles can drive away evil spirits.

In some cultures, people fear crocodilians both because the reptiles might hurt them and because they attack people's pets and livestock (Figure 109). These people kill every crocodilian possible to make the environment "safe."

Some scholars believe that the snake was the first animal symbol. Virtually all human cultures, even those in whose environment snakes are not found, have snake symbols. Snakes

Figure 109. American crocodiles are potentially dangerous to people. Although there are no substantiated reports of attacks on people in the United States, there have been attacks on people further south, including in Mexico, Costa Rica, and Guatemala.

symbolize both good and evil. They feature prominently in creation myths worldwide, but they are also associated with death.

The ancient Greeks viewed snakes as a symbol of renewal and health. By shedding its skin, a snake becomes young and well again. The Greeks portrayed their god of healing, Asclepius, holding a staff with a snake coiled around it. Still today, the staff with its coiled snake is a symbol for the medical profession. Even today, snakes symbolize rejuvenation and immortality because they throw off their old skin and have a fresh one waiting underneath.

Cobras have been worshipped in India and Pakistan for thousands of years (Figure 110). The snakes are believed to have the power to make women fertile and ensure bountiful crops.

Figure 110. For the Hindus of India, the king cobra is the Snake God. This god symbolizes humans' relationship with the cycle of life and death. Hindus pray to the Snake God for protection. King cobras are highly respected for their potent venom.

The Hopis from northern Arizona believe that snakes are messengers between humans and spirits. Hopis live in a bone-dry high desert area. They use snakes to carry their prayers for rain to the gods. Each August, Snake Priests catch bull snakes, desert striped racers, and rattlesnakes from their fields. During the nine-day sacred ceremony, the Hopis wash and bless the snakes. The final festivity is the Snake Dance, during which the Snake Priests dance while holding live snakes in their mouths. After the dance, the snakes are sprinkled with cornmeal. Finally, the men release the snakes to carry their prayers for rain to the gods. Tradition says that the snakes allow the Hopis to live in the high plateau desert by bringing rain. Otherwise, Hopis could not grow corn and other crops in such a dry place.

During the American Revolutionary War (1775–1783) the forefathers of what would become the United States of America used rattlesnakes on flags, with the motto: "Don't Tread on Me." Rattlesnakes symbolized vigilance, deadly striking power, and ethics because they warn before striking. Rattlesnakes don't start fights, but once engaged they don't back down. Likewise, the 13 colonies had no intention of surrendering their independence to Great Britain.

Snakes cause negative reactions too, an attitude that goes back a long time. In the Book of Genesis in the Old Testament of the Bible, the serpent (snake) encourages Eve to eat the fruit that God has forbidden her. She gives some to Adam, and he also eats it. As a result, God expells Adam and Eve, the first two humans He created, from the Garden of Eden. They become mortal, meaning they will eventually die. As for the serpent, God curses it, saying:

> Because you have done this,
>> cursed are you above all cattle,
>> and above all wild animals;
> upon your belly you shall go,
>> and dust you shall eat
>> all the days of your life.

Some people point to this passage of the Bible as their excuse for believing that snakes are evil. Polls taken today indicate that North Americans fear snakes even more than they fear spiders, mice, or speaking in public. Fear of snakes can lead people to kill every one they see (Figure 111).

In Greek mythology, Medusa was very proud of her long, flowing hair. She bragged of her beauty to Athena, goddess of warfare and wisdom. In a jealous rage, Athena turned Medusa into an ugly creature. Medusa became covered with scales, her teeth turned to boar-like tusks, and her hair became writhing snakes. Medusa became so monstrous that anyone who looked at her turned to stone. What a bad rep for snakes!

Figure 111. Some people might kill this harmless milk snake, thinking it is a venomous coral snake. Other people kill any snake they see, out of fear.

Legend has it that Saint Patrick rid Ireland of snakes in the AD 400s when he brought Christianity to the island. He herded all the snakes to the ocean, where they drowned. Snakes symbolized evil in the pagan Druid religion that worshipped many gods and performed animal sacrifices. By introducing Christianity, Patrick got rid of the evil, pagan ways — he drove out the snakes. In reality, Ireland never had any snakes. The only way for them to get there would be by human introduction because the island is surrounded by icy ocean water.

In Baltic mythology hell is an icy hall full of snakes. Venom constantly drips from the snakes' fangs and forms a poisonous river. The damned are forced to swim in this river for eternity. Another negative image for snakes!

Why is it important to know how people feel about amphibians and reptiles? Because once we understand, we can work to change negative attitudes. Once people appreciate amphibians and reptiles they'll be more willing to protect them.

Perhaps the greatest problem is that many people don't think about amphibians and reptiles at all. Like the trees, the air, the oceans and rivers, and like other animals, they are "just there." We go about our lives thinking only of what we need now, and we take amphibians and reptiles for granted. But this is a luxury we can no longer afford.

The world needs these animals. Increasingly people are figuring out how to share the environment with amphibians and reptiles.

14

We Can Live Together, Can't We?

The single most important way we can help amphibians and reptiles is by protecting the environment. How can we do this when there are so many human demands on the land? By compromising. And by suggesting alternatives. Realistically, it's difficult to change the behavior of people associated with commercial logging and mining operations. But we can influence the way individuals use their land.

Conservationists can't demand that people stop slash-and-burn agriculture in order to save the rain forest. Conservationists must consider the needs of the local people. Perhaps slash-and-burn agriculture is the only way the colonists know how to support their families. If they learn alternative ways of earning a living, perhaps they could stop destroying the rain forest. Local people must see habitat protection as a benefit to them if it is going to work.

Conservationists are currently working with people in local communities, experimenting with alternative ways of earning a living in the rain forest without cutting down trees. Nuts are being harvested and carved into buttons and decorative figurines (Figure 112). Fruits and nuts are being gathered for

Figure 112. Selling figurines carved from tagua palm nuts (sometimes called "vegetable ivory") provides a living for indigenous peoples living in the rain forests of Central and South America.

food. Oils and fibers are being extracted from trees. Once trees are viewed as more valuable if left unharmed, the forest will remain intact.

Preservation of Land

When possible, it's ideal to set aside huge areas of land. Governments and conservation organizations can buy land for national parks and reserves. It's not enough to set the land aside, however. The park or reserve, as well as the plants and animals within the boundaries, must be protected from poachers, loggers, and miners. It's getting harder to buy up big tracts of forest because of increasing human demands on the land.

In the United States, National Wildlife Refuges are the only network of federal lands and waters that are managed mainly for the protection of animals. Most of the refuges were established to protect birds and mammals, but at least 9 were set up mainly with amphibians and reptiles in mind:

- Coachella Valley National Wildlife Refuge, California: protection of Coachella Valley fringe-toed lizard

- Ellicott Slough National Wildlife Refuge, California: protection of Santa Cruz long-toed salamander

- Archie Carr National Wildlife Refuge, Florida: protection of green turtle and loggerhead sea turtle (Figure 113)

- Crocodile Lake National Wildlife Refuge, Florida: protection of American crocodile

- Hobe Sound National Wildlife Refuge, Florida; protection of loggerhead sea turtle and green turtle

- Massasoit National Wildlife Refuge, Massachusetts: protection of Plymouth red-bellied turtle

- Mortenson Lake National Wildlife Refuge, Wyoming: protection of Wyoming toad

- Green Cay National Wildlife Refuge, U.S. Virgin Islands; protection of Saint Croix ground lizard

- Sandy Point National Wildlife Refuge, U.S. Virgin Islands; protection of leatherback sea turtle

One reason tropical forests are cut down is that developing countries sell off their forests for lumber to get quick cash to pay off their debts. Developing countries borrow money from international banks to fund projects such as building dams and roads. Worldwide, developing countries owe these banks over 1.5 trillion dollars. When time to repay their loans, the easiest way is often to exploit natural resources, such as forests. Because of severe economic problems, many of these countries will never be able to repay these loans.

Figure 113. Hatchling loggerhead sea turtles have a better chance of surviving thanks to the Archie Carr National Wildlife Refuge in Florida.

Conservationists suggested the "debt-for-nature swap" program in the mid-1980s as a partial solution to this predicament. The program works as follows. A conservation organization works with a developing country to design a conservation project. For example, the project might be to protect a tract of rain forest where endangered monkeys live. The conservation organization buys part of the debt of that developing country at a greatly discounted price from the banks. The banks are willing to do this because they know they'll never see the debt repaid by the developing country. The developing country doesn't have to pay back this part of the debt. In return, the country supports preservation of the land for the monkeys. Many amphibians, reptiles, and other animals that live in the rain forest will be protected also.

The first of these debt-for-nature swaps began in Bolivia, in 1987. In return for not having to pay back $650,000 of the money it owed, Bolivia created the Beni Biosphere Reserve. These 3.7 million acres of rain forest provide protection for parrots, macaws, jaguars, monkeys, anacondas, side-necked turtles, treefrogs, caecilians, and all the other animals and plants in the area (Figure 114). Conservation International bought the Bolivian debt for a mere $100,000. Since then, debt-for-nature swaps have been carried out in other countries, including Ecuador, Peru, Costa Rica, Mexico, the Philippine Islands, and Madagascar.

One way of protecting private land in the United States is through *conservation easements*. These are agreements on how private land will be used. The agreement is made between the

Figure 114. Anacondas are just one of many reptiles protected in the Beni Biosphere Reserve in Bolivia.

government or a conservation organization and the landowner. If the land is especially valuable for plants and animals, the landowner receives money or perhaps a tax benefit in return for not developing the land. Here's how this might work:

A rancher owns 1000 acres of cattle pasture. His other 200 acres are swampland, which he's considering selling to a developer. The swamp would be filled in with sand and converted to a shopping mall. Residents of the town nearby would like the mall, and the rancher wouldn't mind having the extra money. But, he feels guilty because he promised his granddad that he would keep the land undeveloped. The local conservation organization argues against development because rare salamanders live in the swamp. The rancher and members of the conservation group strike a deal: they set up a conservation easement. In return for not developing the land, the rancher receives a lump sum of money. The protected land benefits not only the rare salamanders but also all the other plants and animals that live there. Everyone is happy, except the townspeople who didn't get their mall.

Sharing Earth

Some amphibians and reptiles, such as Komodo dragons, require huge areas of land away from people. To protect Komodo dragons, we need to set aside land for them.

Other amphibians and reptiles have life styles more compatible with the presence of people. In fact some *species*, like Grenada Bank treeboas, thrive in human-disturbed areas. As their name suggests, these boas are *arboreal*.

Figure 115. Bob Henderson has studied Grenada Bank treeboas on Grenada for over 20 years.

Bob Henderson has found that these treeboas live in edge habitats on the Caribbean island of Grenada (Figure 115). They occur in natural vegetation, such as along edges of rain forest, and also along edges of fruit orchards — mango, cacao, citrus, breadfruit, and nutmeg. Bob thinks that the planting of these trees has provided more edge habitat for the snakes, allowing them to increase in numbers and expand their range.

Not only have the treeboas adapted to human-induced changes in the landscape, but also they have adapted to different prey and predators associated with people. Before Europeans arrived on Grenada about 500 years ago, the treeboas probably ate *Anolis* lizards and two species of rice rats. These mammals are now extinct. Now the treeboas eat introduced mice and black rats in addition to lizards. Prior to the arrival of Europeans, the snakes' primary predators were probably raptors (birds of prey), such as broad-winged hawks. Now, in addition to native raptors, the snakes' predators are introduced opossums and possibly introduced mongoose and Mona monkeys. And yet, Bob finds that the snakes are doing well living near people. They forage for food at the edges of lighted parking lots, and they cross roads on power lines. Now that's an *adaptable* species!

We need to change how we use the environment so we can coexist better with certain amphibians and reptiles. Following are some examples of how we can do this.

We Can Help Animals to Cross Roads Safely. Some toads live in the forest most of the year. After heavy rains in the spring, they migrate to ponds and lay their eggs. Afterward, the toads return to the forest where they stay until the next breeding season. What happens if a road is built between the forest and the pond? To get to the pond, the toads will have to cross the road. Many will never make it to the other side. They'll be squashed by cars and trucks.

Australian scientists estimate that nearly 5.5 million amphibians and reptiles are killed on paved roads each year in their country! Imagine how many are squashed on roads every year throughout the world. Just in the United States, we have

4 million miles of public roads. Over 254 million passenger vehicles travel these roads.

Concerned citizens have developed ways of reducing the numbers of animals killed on roads. In some areas in Europe and North America, road signs warn motorists about migrations of toads and salamanders. Motorists are asked not to use these roads during the toad and salamander breeding seasons. If the roads must be used, motorists are asked to drive slowly and avoid the animals.

In some places engineers build tunnels under roads to connect critical habitats for amphibians and reptiles (Figure 116). They construct barriers along both sides of the road so that animals can't walk, hop, crawl, or slither onto the pavement. The animals turn right or left and follow along the barrier until they find an opening — the tunnel. Once through the tunnel, they've safely crossed the road and can continue on their way. These tunnels have prevented the slaughter of many thousands of frogs, toads, salamanders, snakes, and turtles.

Where there are no tunnels, human volunteers can do the job. Adults and kids collect toads in buckets and carry them safely across roads. They call themselves "toad patrols." In the United Kingdom, toad patrols at more than 400 sites save an estimated 500,000 toads each year. Some communities in Canada and the United States also have toad patrols. Get your friends together and form a toad patrol. It's fun!

We Can Dig Ponds for Amphibians. People try to simplify their lives, but in the process other animals sometimes get hurt. For example, in one area of the Netherlands much of the

Figure 116. This tunnel that runs under the road is one of the first constructed in Massachusetts to help amphibians cross roads safely.

land is used for cattle pastures. In the early 1900s, the area had over 1000 cattle-watering ponds. Salamanders and frogs used these ponds for breeding. During the past 40 years, ranchers have replaced many of these ponds with concrete drinking basins and automatic self-drink devices for the cattle. With fewer breeding ponds, two of the 12 species of amphibians once present have disappeared and another five are declining. Fortunately, concerned people have come to the rescue. They're digging new ponds for the amphibians.

Midwife toads in Spain also have declined because ranchers have replaced cattle-watering ponds with modern watering

Figure 117. It would be sad to lose midwife toads. The five species of midwife toads are special in their unique parental care behavior.

devices (Figure 117). Midwife toads get their name because the males carry the eggs entwined around their waists and thighs until the eggs are just about ready to hatch. At that point the males hop into shallow water and the hatchlings burst forth from their egg capsules. If there's no water available for the father to hop into, the eggs dry up and die before they can hatch. Help is on the way, though. Men, women, and children are digging ponds for the toads.

Do you know an area that could use a frog pond? If so, begin by talking with your teacher. Perhaps he or she can organize a class project.

We Can Turn Out the Lights for Baby Turtles. Female sea turtles crawl out of the ocean and lay their eggs in holes they dig on the beach. The eggs incubate in the warm sand, and eventually the baby turtles hatch. The hatchlings usually dig their way out at night and make a beeline for the ocean. How do they know which way the water is? Hatchling turtles instinctively head for the brightest horizon. Normally the brightest light comes from moonlight or starlight reflected off the surface of the ocean. When people build homes close to the ocean, the lights shining from these buildings confuse baby turtles. Instead of heading for the ocean, the hatchlings head inland, toward the lights from the buildings. Many dry up in the sun the next day or are run over by cars and trucks.

Many communities along the beaches of the southeastern United States now have rules about turning lights off during the sea turtle nesting season. For example, along turtle nesting beaches in Florida, lights are generally allowed only until 11:00 at night. After 11:00 p.m., without artificial lights to confuse them, the baby turtles orient correctly and make it to the ocean. The ones that emerge before 11:00 p.m. are the unlucky ones.

We Can Help Sea Turtles Escape from Shrimp Nets. In the United States, a major cause of death for sea turtles is from drowning in the nets that fishermen use to catch shrimp. In fact, more sea turtles die in these nets than from all other human-caused sources of death combined. Some years more than 60,000 die in shrimp nets. Once entangled in the nets, the turtles can't swim to the surface for air. They often drown in less than an hour.

A clever contraption, called a turtle excluder device (TED), was designed in the early 1980s as a solution. A TED is a small net or metal cage-like device that is sewn into the shrimp net (Figure 118). It allows shrimp to be caught in the net but

Figure 118. Turtle excluder devices (TEDs) have saved the lives of many sea turtles. Enforcing their use is difficult, however. Some shrimpers refuse to use them because they catch fewer shrimp when the TED is in the net.

allows turtles to escape. The turtle's body flips through a trapdoor and back into the ocean. The best TEDs allow about 97% of the turtles caught to escape. Since the mid-1990s, shrimpers in the United States are now required by the federal government to use TEDs, and conservation organizations even offer to pay for them. TEDs are currently used in at least 15 countries. This is just one more way that we can share Earth with amphibians and reptiles.

15
Research and Education

After habitat protection and sharing the environment, the two most important ways we can protect amphibians and reptiles are by learning more about them and by educating people about the importance and value of these animals.

Research

Does anyone reading this book want to be a biologist? A *conservation* biologist? A conservation biologist who works with amphibians and reptiles? For anyone who answered "yes" to these questions, there's a lot of work waiting for you.

We need more research to understand how we can best protect amphibians and reptiles. This includes gathering information about what they eat and who eats them; about their social behavior, reproductive patterns, and habitat preferences; about the sizes of their *populations*; and about the natural and human-caused factors that are responsible for their declining populations.

In order to protect habitat for a certain *species*, we need to know what habitat that species uses. Does it spend all of its life in the forest? Does it migrate between swampland and forest? Research will answer these questions.

Semi-*aquatic* turtles live in wetlands. They spend much of their time in the water, but they wander to higher ground to lay their eggs on land. Federal laws protect wetlands and a little dry land around them by prohibiting development within the area. Scientists have found, however, that sometimes not enough land is protected as a buffer zone.

Research on turtles in a wetland in South Carolina showed that all of the turtles' nesting sites and all of their hibernation burrows were on dry land outside the protected area (Figure 119). Obviously, the laws were not adequate for protecting these turtles. What if a developer had built an apartment complex near the wetland — the perfect place for residents to watch turtles basking on logs? Where would the turtles lay their eggs? Where would they hibernate in the winter? Now that research has shown that the turtles need more land for their nesting and hibernation activities, conservation biologists can argue that the federal regulations need to be changed.

We also need research to be sure we're protecting the right stages of animals. To protect sea turtles, should we focus on the eggs, baby turtles, or adults? To determine which age group needs the most protection, we need information on the chance of dying and the major causes of death at each stage. Sea turtles live a long time. Each female lays hundreds of eggs, but predators eat most of the eggs and baby turtles. In some species, fewer than 1% of the eggs become adult turtles. Since so many eggs and baby turtles will die no matter what, conservation efforts should focus mainly on sub-adults and adults.

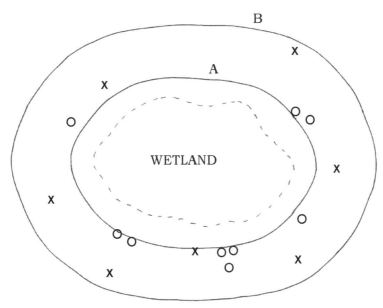

Figure 119. The area inside the broken lines represents a wetland where turtles live. During warm weather, these turtles spend much of their time in the water or sunning on logs. They move farther away from the water to lay their eggs and hibernate during the winter. United States wetland laws protect the area enclosed by ring A. As you can see, these turtles are at risk if a developer builds an apartment complex that includes area in between ring A and ring B. The Os represent nesting sites, and the Xs represent hibernation sites.

We learned this lesson the hard way with Kemp's ridley (Figure 120). Biologists spent over 14 years (1978–1992) and more than $4 million protecting eggs on the nesting beach in Mexico, transporting the eggs to the United States, and then raising the young in a laboratory safe from predators. Over time, the biologists released more than 20,000 babies (9–12 months old) into the coastal waters of Texas and Florida. But after all those years of protection, there weren't many more

Figure 120. Kemp's ridleys are the world's most endangered sea turtles.

Kemp's ridleys than when the project began. Why? Because so many adult turtles drown in shrimp nets. The best way to protect Kemp's ridleys is to require shrimp fishermen to use turtle excluder devices. Fishermen in the United States are now required to do so, and as of 1993 Mexico now requires its shrimp fishermen in the Gulf of Mexico and Caribbean waters to use TEDs. Life is looking up for Kemp's ridleys. In 2006, a record number of nests were observed since monitoring began in 1978.

For many species of amphibians and reptiles we don't know how much space individuals need to carry out their daily activities, such as foraging for food. If we want to set aside land to protect anacondas, we'll need a much larger area than if we wish to set aside land for an *endangered* salamander. But how much more land?

How many individual anacondas must there be in the preserve for them to find each other and breed successfully? How many individual salamanders do we need in our smaller preserve for them to breed successfully? These are questions that can be answered only with more research.

Scientists worldwide are carrying out research to unravel what's going on with the worldwide declines and disappearances of amphibians and reptiles. They're establishing long-term monitoring programs to document which species are declining, and they're studying the possible causes of observed declines.

Education

"Please Brake for Snakes" reads the diamond-shaped sign posted in Killbear Provincial Park in Ontario, Canada. The sign reaches out to park visitors as part of a project to promote conservation of the eastern massasauga rattlesnake (Figure 121). These shy and non-aggressive snakes are declining in Ontario and the United States because people are destroying their habitat and killing the snakes. In Killbear Provincial Park, as many rattlesnakes are killed by cars as are eaten by natural predators. Thus the sign.

Park personnel offer snake talks for campers. People's attitudes quickly change from fear to respect. People come into the talk thinking that rattlesnakes lie in wait for the chance to strike people. They leave the talk realizing that instead of these snakes threatening us, we are threatening them. The conservation message is that the 250,000 yearly human visitors to

Figure 121. The eastern massasauga rattlesnake is Ontario's only venomous snake.

the park can safely coexist with the 200 to 300 rattlesnakes that live there.

The rattlesnake education project has been extremely successful. Many residents of the area who once killed every rattlesnake they saw, now carefully sweep the snakes into over-turned garbage cans. They call the park staff so that data can be collected on the locations and activities of the snakes. Most amazing is the cooperation from visitors to the park. When campers report a rattlesnake, the park staff catch it and record data. Afterward, the staff ask the campers for permission to relocate the snake within 500 yards (sometimes less than 100 yards) of its capture site. The campers have veto power, but they nearly always agree to the release. Thanks to what they've learned about rattlesnakes, the campers know that the snake makes that area its home and that's where it should be. That's an effective education program!

Recently, many countries have realized that tourists will pay lots of money to see native wildlife. Tourists pay entrance fees to visit a reserve. They spend money on hiring local guides, buying food and souvenirs, and staying in local hotels. All of this enriches the local economy. So, instead of allowing timber companies to cut down their forests, governments and local communities are setting aside protected land and encouraging *ecotourism* — tourism based on natural history.

Africa has some of the world's most popular nature reserves, where you can see lions, giraffes, and zebras. But ecotourism focusing on amphibians and reptiles is also popular. You can go to Costa Rica or Florida and watch sea turtles come ashore to lay their eggs. You can travel to the exotic island of Komodo in Indonesia and watch Komodo dragons go about their daily activities (Figure 122). Another popular activity for ecotourists is photographing marine iguanas and giant tortoises on the Galápagos Islands off the coast of Ecuador.

Ecotourism provides a great opportunity to educate the public both about the animals they're watching and the need for conservation of these animals and their habitats. Carefully controlled ecotourism can protect habitat and wildlife and at the same time improve people's attitudes about nature. Ecotourism also provides a unique opportunity for local people

Figure 122. This ecotourist is enjoying her experience on Komodo Island!

to participate in the teaching as well as the learning part of the education process. Local people can help construct displays, distribute pamphlets and newsletters, produce radio and television programs, and work as guides and park guards in their reserve.

Another way of educating the public is to include non-scientists in research projects, such as monitoring the status of endangered or declining amphibians and reptiles. In one Canadian project, pairs of people monitor the number of frogs at breeding sites. Each pair surveys its pond one rainy night per month. It's great fun for the participants, and many more ponds are surveyed than if one investigator were to do it alone. Once non-scientists become involved, they become more interested in the animals and the need to protect their habitats. They spread the word and educate others.

Non-scientists are needed as volunteers throughout the world to help with conservation projects. One exciting opportunity involves the Utila iguana, a large lizard found only on the island of Utila, off the coast of Honduras in Central America. This spiny-tailed iguana is threatened with extinction, largely because local people hunt the pregnant females and eat their eggs. Scientists have developed an extensive public education program, which includes a field station, to teach the locals about their unique iguana and the importance of not hunting them. Since 1994, more than 500 volunteers have helped in many phases of the project, including field research, educating the public, and caring for captive iguanas at the field station.

You don't need to visit foreign countries to learn about amphibians and reptiles and their need for conservation. And you don't need to help a scientist with his or her study. You can watch amphibians and reptiles in your own backyard or nearby woods (Figure 123). When you have questions, go to the library or talk with your parents or your teacher. Share what you learn with others. The more educated you become, the more you can convince others of the importance of conserving these animals.

Figure 123. Wouldn't it be fun to observe long-tailed salamanders in nature? These salamanders live near streams and in wetlands in much of the eastern United States. During the day you'll find them under logs and rocks. At night they wander around on the ground and forage for small invertebrates.

There are other ways to help as well . . .

16

What Else Can Be Done?

Although habitat protection, research, and education are critical, there are additional ways of protecting amphibians and reptiles. Laws can be effective if they're rigidly enforced. We can move animals into areas where *populations* of a particular *species* have disappeared. Instead of collecting amphibians and reptiles from the wild and killing them for skins or food or selling them for pets, we can raise animals in captivity. We can use fewer animals for dissections. We can regulate legal hunting of amphibians and reptiles so that populations don't decline or go extinct.

Laws That Protect Amphibians and Reptiles

Countries vary in how much they protect amphibians and reptiles. Some countries protect no species at all. At the other extreme, in Belgium all amphibians and reptiles except for two common species of frogs have been protected for over 35 years. Laws aren't enough, though. They must be enforced.

In 1973, the United States passed the Endangered Species Act, a law that protects both domestic and foreign wildlife classified as either *endangered* or *threatened* (Figure 124). Endangered species are those that are in danger of extinction throughout all or most of their ranges. Threatened species are those that are likely to become endangered within the near future. Once a species is listed as either endangered or threatened, scientists develop a recovery plan. This plan might involve buying and preserving critical habitat, breeding the species in captivity, relocating animals to a different area, and/or doing additional research.

As of 2011, 33 species of amphibians and 119 reptiles are protected under the United States Endangered Species Act. Of these, 101 are considered endangered and 51 are considered threatened. If a person is caught killing or taking an endangered or threatened species from the wild, he or she can be fined or thrown into jail — unless that person has a permit for scientific study. The Endangered Species Act also protects critical

Figure 124. Komodo dragons are currently protected as an endangered species by the Endangered Species Act.

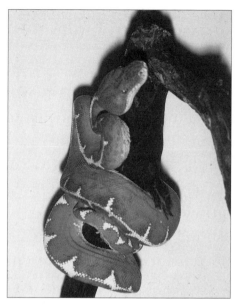

Figure 125. All boas, including this emerald tree boa, are protected by CITES.

habitat needed by endangered and threatened species. It's against the law to destroy habitat used by protected species.

Also in 1973, an international endangered species treaty was drafted by 81 nations — the Convention on International Trade in Endangered Species of Wild Fauna and Flora (CITES). The CITES treaty protects wildlife and plants throughout the world by declaring it illegal to sell endangered species, live or dead, to another country. Because it is now illegal to import endangered species, poachers have no legal market for their illegally captured animals (Figure 125). The CITES treaty also protects species that biologists think might become endangered. These species can be collected and sold only if the proper permits are obtained. As of 2011, 175 countries have signed the CITES treaty. The treaty currently protects about 5000 species of animals and 28,000 species of plants. Protected under CITES are 657 species of reptiles and 114 species of amphibians. A few examples are the harlequin poison frog (Plate 12), Japanese giant salamander (Plate 13), Gila monster (Plate 4), Jackson's chameleon (Plate 8), Komodo dragon (Plate 8), and rainbow boa (Plate 3). Unfortunately, CITES deals only with buying and selling of wildlife across international borders. It does not apply to trade within countries.

These laws sound good, but once again they're only as good as their enforcement. And they are difficult to enforce. About 30% of the world's trade in wildlife is estimated to be in violation of CITES and national laws. Examples include endangered tortoises smuggled into the United States and Europe from Madagascar for the pet trade. Shoes, boots, and handbags made from smuggled snake and crocodilian skin. Tortoiseshell (*scutes* from hawksbill sea turtles) smuggled into Japan to be carved into jewelry and other objects. Turtles smuggled into China for meat and folk medicines.

Reestablish Populations in the Wild

Sometimes when a population disappears, we can move animals from elsewhere and reestablish the population.

Imagine the following scene in southern California. The ground is dry and hard. The ponds are basins of cracked mud (Figure 126). Two years ago was a record dry summer. The following summer was almost as dry. An endangered treefrog has disappeared from the area. The third summer,

Figure 126. Sometimes during periods of drought, ponds dry up and amphibians that lay aquatic eggs must go elsewhere to breed.

rains return in full force. The ponds fill with water, but no treefrogs come to breed. Is this population gone forever? Not necessarily.

Frogs might migrate in from nearby areas and colonize these ponds on their own. If not, people can collect frogs from nearby areas and release them at the site. This makes sense if the reason for the disappearance is a natural event, such as unusual weather. But would it make sense to relocate animals to an area that was formerly a forest but is now a subdivision packed with homes? No. Can you think of other instances where it wouldn't make sense to try and reestablish populations?

Gopher tortoises live in dry, sandy areas in the coastal plains of the United States between South Carolina and Louisiana. They dig and live in burrows about 13 feet long. Because they need dry areas for their burrows, the tortoises prefer land that humans also want for building their homes and shopping malls. Humans are more powerful, so we take the land and displace the tortoises. As a result, populations of gopher tortoises are dwindling, even though the Endangered Species Act protects these tortoises in much of their range.

What's a developer to do if gopher tortoises live on land he or she plans to convert to condominiums? Some states require the developer to move the tortoises to another appropriate habitat. Biologists choose substitute areas based on knowledge of the tortoises' feeding and habitat requirements, and then they relocate the tortoises.

Moving wild animals from one place to another isn't always a solution, however. One problem is that sometimes the animals don't stay where we put them. They wander off until they find what they consider to be prime real estate. Another problem, especially if the animals have spent time in captivity, is that the former captives can spread disease to wild animals.

One way of reestablishing populations, called *head-starting*, involves hatching eggs in captivity. The hatchlings are raised to a size large enough so that when they're released into the wild they'll be less likely to be eaten by predators. Scientists are currently using head-starting programs to reestablish populations of some amphibians, lizards, turtles and tortoises, crocodilians, and tuatara.

Figure 127. Baby Galápagos tortoises are raised from eggs in incubators. The babies are housed in outdoor pens until they are large enough that most predators can't eat them. At that point, usually between the ages of 4 and 5 years, they are released into the wild.

One success story is work being done at the Charles Darwin Research Station in the Galápagos Islands. There, workers raise tortoises and land iguanas from eggs (Figure 127). Once the young reptiles grow to a reasonable size, the workers release them onto islands where predators are controlled. So far, the efforts seem to be working. Populations of tortoises and land iguanas are increasing on these islands.

Another success story is a head-starting project with Utila iguanas on Utila Island, off the coast of Honduras, in Central America. In addition to the education program mentioned in

Chapter Fifteen, biologists are breeding the lizards. Workers catch pregnant females from the nesting beaches and put them in large cages with sand. After the females lay their eggs, the workers set the lizards free. Safe from predators, most of the artificially incubated eggs hatch. The workers release half of the hatchlings in the mangrove swamps immediately. They raise the other half at the breeding station for a year, and then release them when they're large enough to be less vulnerable to predators such as birds, snakes, dogs, and cats.

One of the only two species of tuatara, the Brother Island tuatara, is found naturally only on North Brother Island. The population is estimated at about 400 individuals. Wildlife biologists have head-started this species and released hatchlings onto other islands as a safeguard against extinction. Just in case all go extinct in the wild, the San Diego Zoo has a colony of Brother Island tuatara that it cares for in an off-exhibit area (Figure 128).

Captive Raising of Animals for Skins, Food, and Pets

Instead of killing or collecting wild animals for skins, food, or pets, we can raise the animals in captivity. Once they're large enough the animals can be sold.

There are two types of such businesses: farms and ranches. In a *farming operation*, people initially collect adult animals from the wild. They breed the adults on the farm and raise the eggs. The owners set aside some of the young for future breeding stock, and they kill and sell the rest. Unfortunately, because the farmers don't need any more animals from

Figure 128. This Brother Island tuatara lives in the San Diego Zoo.

the wild, they have no incentive to protect wild populations or their natural habitat.

In a *ranching operation*, workers take eggs or hatchlings from the wild and raise them in captivity to be sold later. Each year or so they collect more eggs or hatchlings from the wild. Because ranching depends on a continuing supply of wild animals, there is strong incentive to protect both the habitat and wild populations.

There are some success stories. Farms and ranches in Africa are producing high quality skins of Nile crocodiles. Eventually there should be enough skins from captive animals so that wild crocodiles will no longer be hunted.

Costa Ricans farm green iguanas and release the captive-raised juveniles into areas where the lizards have been hunted out. Two or three years later, people can hunt these iguanas for food. The project provides two benefits: *conservation* of declining populations of green iguanas, and incentive to protect the tropical forest. If people want the young iguanas to grow large enough so they can hunt them, they've got to provide food — leaves from the treetops (Figure 129).

People are now captive-breeding many amphibians and reptiles popular as pets. Some of these include poison frogs, horned frogs, leopard geckos, green iguanas, chameleons, bearded dragon lizards, pythons, and boas.

Not all animals can be raised in captivity successfully, though. Frog farming was once thought to be a way of satisfying the world's craving for frog legs. Bullfrog farms became

Figure 129. Adult green iguanas are herbivorous. They eat leaves, flowers, and fruits.

Figure 130. Not only do bullfrogs have voracious appetites, but also they eat large prey — turtles, snakes, birds, rodents, and other bullfrogs.

popular in the United States, Japan, Brazil, Ecuador, Argentina, and other countries. Bullfrogs grow very slowly, however, and it's hard to provide enough live food to satisfy bullfrogs' voracious appetites (Figure 130). For these reasons, it's expensive to farm frogs and few operations have been successful. Most frog legs destined for the table are still caught in the wild.

Fewer Dissections

Every year there is less demand for wild-caught amphibians used for classroom dissections. In part this is because more animals are being raised in laboratories for educational purposes. Another factor is that teachers are becoming more aware that amphibians are declining. There's no need for every student to do a dissection. Now, students often work in groups. Many states in the United States and many western

European countries now have "dissection-choice" laws. Students are given the option of not dissecting animals. Argentina and the Slovak Republic have actually banned dissection of animals in high schools!

There are also alternatives to dissection. Videotapes of frog dissections can be used. CD-ROMs are available. You can dissect 3-dimensional frog models. And you can even go to the Web to *www.froguts.com* and dissect a frog by moving your mouse.

Wiser Harvesting of Wild Populations

People who think we should protect all wildlife would support laws banning the killing of all animals in the name of conservation. At the other extreme, some people believe that it's their right to hunt whatever animals they want, and as many as they want. Conservation biologists believe that for many species of wildlife we can both conserve and hunt them.

The key is that harvesting (removing animals from wild populations) must be done on a sustainable basis. *Sustainable harvesting* means removing individuals from a population in such a way that the population will be there long into the future. This might mean taking only a few individuals from the population, or taking only "extra" adult males and leaving the females.

Many conservation biologists support the harvest of wildlife on a sustainable basis because it gives countries an incentive to protect their wildlife and critical habitats. For example, because legally-caught crocodilian skins are worth a lot of

Figure 131. This baby caiman has a much greater chance of getting eaten by a predator than does an adult caiman.

money, many countries protect wetlands and carefully regulate hunting so that crocodilian populations are not wiped out. Every crocodile, alligator, or caiman is worth money!

How do we know which animals to remove and how many we can remove to practice sustainable harvesting? Only research can provide these answers. Biologists carry out long-term studies to determine the number of juveniles, subadults, and adults in a population. They study the causes of death and the chance of an individual surviving to maturity (Figure 131). They learn how many eggs a female produces during a breeding season and how often females breed per lifetime. Once armed with solid data, biologists can make recommendations so that collecting or hunting can be done without causing the population to go extinct.

∾

YOU can help too . . .

17

What Can YOU Do to Help?

When we think about all the ways that humans are responsible for the declines and disappearances of amphibians and reptiles, it's easy to become discouraged. But when we think about all the positive steps people are taking, or can take, to protect these animals, we have reason to be hopeful.

YOU can be part of the solution. *Conservation*-minded young adults are often more receptive to new ideas than are adults. YOU are the generation that can have a major impact on the future of amphibians and reptiles, beginning now. YOU will be the voters of tomorrow. YOU will be setting the policies of tomorrow. YOU will raise the children of tomorrow. YOU can make a difference.

Below are some ideas of things to do — and things not to do — to help amphibians and reptiles.

DON'T!

- Don't destroy habitat. Habitat modification and destruction are the major causes of declines and disappearances of amphibians and reptiles. If you're out in the woods looking for amphibians and reptiles, be sure to put the rocks and logs back in place after you've looked underneath them.

216

- Don't release exotic amphibians and reptiles into the environment (Figure 132). They might eat local amphibians and reptiles. Or they could survive and breed, eventually out-competing local amphibians and reptiles for food or habitat. Find someone who will care for the animals and enjoy them as you once did.

- Don't buy souvenirs made from amphibians and reptiles. Key chains made from rattlesnake rattles may look cool, but the rattles belong to the snakes. Cowboy

Figure 132. This comical-looking animal is a White's tree frog from Australia, commonly sold in pet stores. If one of these frogs gets loose, it might eat smaller native tree frogs.

boots made from tegu lizard skins are beautiful, but even more beautiful is a live tegu basking on a log. You may be tempted to buy an exquisitely carved tortoiseshell object in a foreign country. Don't. Not only was a sea turtle killed to make the object, but also it's illegal to bring tortoiseshell into the United States. Don't eat sea turtle soup or the meat of any other *endangered* reptile or amphibian. The less we support the exploitation of amphibians and reptiles, the fewer animals will be killed and made into souvenirs or gourmet dishes.

DO!

- Do educate yourself about amphibians and reptiles. The more you learn about them, the more you'll appreciate them and the more you'll want to protect them (Figure 133). Read. Your library has good books about these animals. If there's a *herpetological* club in your city, join it. You'll meet other people who share your interests. Many local museums, zoos, and nature centers offer classes on amphibians and reptiles. Spend time outdoors observing amphibians and reptiles in their natural environment. Keep a notebook and record your observations. You may discover something new to science.

- Do volunteer your time. Often scientists working in universities, museums, or nature centers use volunteer help. You can dig ponds for amphibians in areas where natural breeding ponds have been destroyed. During rainy spring and summer evenings you can help migrating amphibians and reptiles to cross roads safely. You can help monitor *populations*. Check out the websites listed in the back of the book for ideas of how

Figure 133. The Red Hills salamander is one species in need of protection. Only just "discovered" in 1960, we know of only 13 populations of the species — all in Alabama.

you can volunteer your time. For example, during 2010–2011, the Save the Frogs organization sponsored a "Build a Frog Pond" contest. School children, homeowners, and other interested people were invited to build frog ponds on their property. People documented their projects and their successes through video, photographs, and stories posted online. The information educated and inspired readers to do the same.

- Do let people know that conserving amphibians and reptiles is important. You can improve the public image of these animals by letting others know how fascinating they are. Give talks to your classmates at school. Write letters to the editor for your local newspaper. Often when a *threatened species* is being considered for protection, the public is invited and encouraged to express their viewpoints. Write letters that express your opinions. Send the letters to your state and national representatives, and have all your friends add their signatures. The representatives will be impressed by your knowledge and interest.

- Do support conservation organizations. Begin by reading about the different conservation groups. Some buy land and preserve it. Others spend money to protect wildlife. Others fund research to study threatened and endangered species. Some do a combination of activities. Choose an organization whose goals and activities you most admire. Then ask your parents to give you a membership in your chosen organization. You'll receive a magazine or newsletter, providing you with information on conservation projects and the status of threatened and endangered plants and animals. Another idea: Join Amphibian Ark (AArk), Save the Frogs, or another organization that works to protect amphibians and/or reptiles.

- Do be responsible if you want to keep amphibians and reptiles as pets. Never take a threatened or endangered species from the wild (Figure 134). To find out which species are protected, contact a United States Fish and Wildlife Service officer or check this web site: *www.fws.gov/endangered.* Go to the home page, where you can search the Endangered Species Database. If you're buying an exotic animal from a pet store, ask if it was bred in captivity. Don't buy exotic animals that were taken from the wild. The fewer of these animals

220

Figure 134. Hatchling gopher tortoises are awfully cute. In case you're ever tempted to take one home as a pet, don't. These tortoises are legally protected as either a threatened or endangered species, depending on the state.

that are sold, the fewer will be shipped in future years. Find out about your pet's needs — food, water, habitat, and temperature and moisture conditions — and then provide them with the best substitute home you can.

- Do make your backyard a good place for amphibians and reptiles. Leave rocks or logs on the ground to serve as shelters. Urge your parents to use organic insecticides rather than toxins to kill insect pests that eat your garden vegetables and flowers. This way the amphibians and reptiles in your yard won't die from eating poisoned insects. If you have a cat, keep it indoors or at least don't let it outside unsupervised. Cats are very efficient predators. They can wipe out the lizards in your neighborhood in no time.

221

Figure 135. The future of amphibians and reptiles — including this baby snake-necked turtle — is in our hands.

If we all do our part to help protect the environment and the animals themselves, our grandchildren's grandchildren will be able to learn about amphibians and reptiles from watching them in the wild. If would be sad indeed if frogs, salamanders, caecilians, turtles, crocodilians, lizards, snakes, and tuatara joined the dinosaurs on the growing list of extinct animals.

You and I together can make a difference (Figure 135). Please help.

Appendix I

Additional Resources

Amphibians and Reptiles

Books

Badger, David. *Frogs*. Stillwater, MN: Voyageur Press, Inc., 1995.

Baskin-Salzberg, Anita, and Allen Salzberg. *Turtles*. New York, NY: Franklin Watts, 1996.

Bauchot, Roland (Editor). *Snakes: A Natural History*. New York, NY: Sterling Publishing Co., Inc., 1994.

Behler, John L. *First Field Guide: Reptiles*. National Audubon Society. New York, NY: Scholastic Inc., 1999.

Behler, John L., and Deborah A. Behler. *Alligators and Crocodiles*. Stillwater, MN: Voyageur Press, 1998.

Cassie, Brian. *First Field Guide: Amphibians*. National Audubon Society. New York, NY: Scholastic Inc, 1999.

Cherry, Jim. *Loco for Lizards*. Flagstaff, AZ: Northland Publishing, 2000.

Clarke, Barry. *Eyewitness Books: Amphibian*. New York, NY: Dorling Kindersley Publishing, Inc., 2000.

Crump, Marty. *Mysteries of the Komodo Dragon*. Honesdale, PA: Boyds Mills Press, 2010.

Elliott, Leslee. *Really Radical Reptiles & Amphibians*. New York, NY: Sterling Publishing Co., 1994.

Greer, Allen E. (Consulting Editor). *Reptiles*. Time-Life Books, 1996.

Halliday, Tim R., and Kraig Adler (Editors). *The Encyclopedia of Reptiles and Amphibians*. New York, NY: Facts on File, Inc., 1986.

Johnson, Sylvia A. *Tree Frogs*. Minneapolis, MN: Lerner Publications Company, 1986.

Lamar, William W. *The World's Most Spectacular Reptiles & Amphibians*. Tampa, FL: World Publications, 1997.

Ling, Mary, and Mary Atkinson. *The Snake Book*. New York, NY: Dorling Kindersley, 2000.

Mattison, Chris. *Frogs & Toads of the World*. New York, NY: Facts on File, 1987.

———. *Lizards of the World*. New York, NY: Facts on File, 1989.

———. *Snakes of the World*. New York, NY: Facts on File, 1990.

———. *Snake*. Richmond Hill, ONT: Firefly Books Ltd, 1999.

McCarthy, Colin. *Eyewitness Books: Reptile*. New York, NY: Alfred A. Knopf, 1991.

Owen, Oliver S. *Tadpole to Frog: Lifewatch. The Mystery of Nature*. Edina, MN: Abdo & Daughters, 1994.

Preszler, June. *Scaly Blood Squirters and Other Extreme Reptiles*. Mankato, MN: Capstone Press, 2008.

Sill, Cathryn. *About Amphibians*. Atlanta, GA: Peachtree Publishers, Ltd, 2000.

Simon, Seymour. *Snakes*. New York, NY: HarperCollins Publishers, 1992.

———. *Crocodiles and Alligators*. New York, NY: HarperCollins Publishers, 1999.

Spirn, Michele S. *Ripley's Cold-Blooded Creatures*. New York, NY: Scholastic Inc, 2004.

Tesar, Jenny. *What on Earth Is a Tuatara?* Woodbridge, CT: Blackbirch Press, 1994.

Townsend, John. *Incredible Amphibians*. Mankato, MN: Heinemann-Raintree, 2005.

Twist, Clint. *Reptiles and Amphibians Dictionary: An A to Z of Cold-Blooded Creatures*. New York, NY: Tangerine Press, Scholastic, 2005.

Williams, Brian. *Amazing Reptiles and Amphibians*. Pleasantville, NY: Gareth Stevens Publishing, 2008.

Web Sites

http://amphibianark.org/
   Mission is to ensure the survival of amphibians worldwide, focusing on species that cannot be safeguarded in nature. Species that would otherwise go extinct in nature are maintained in captivity.

http://nationalzoo.si.edu/Animals/ReptilesAmphibians/Facts/default.cfm
   Smithsonian National Zoological Park. Fun facts about amphibians and reptiles; resources for teachers.

http://teacher.scholastic.com/activities/explorations/lizards/
   American Museum of Natural History. Information, teacher resources, and student activities focusing on lizards and snakes.

www.allaboutfrogs.org
   Interesting, weird, and silly facts about frogs; declining amphibian populations; frogs as pets.

www.amphibiaweb.org
   Amphibia Web: information on amphibian biology and conservation; great source for teachers.

www.cgee.hamline.edu/frogs/science/frogfact.html
   A Thousand Friends of Frogs. Information about amphibians, including population declines.

www.froguts.com
   Dissect a frog without killing an animal — move your mouse!

www.homestead.com/kidstuff/index.html
   Pet care, books, and videos about frogs; miscellaneous facts about frogs.

www.naherpetology.org
   The Center for North American Herpetology (CNAH). Announcements of herpetological meetings, publications, links with other herpetological web sites, careers in herpetology; focus is on the United States and Canada.

www.parcplace.org
  Conservation and biology of amphibians and reptiles: threats, conservation efforts, geographic distribution.

www.savethefrogs.com
  Great source of information and suggestions for how you can get involved to help save frogs.

www.sdnhm.org/exhibits/reptiles
  Some information refers to exhibits at the San Diego Natural History Museum, but there are also games and information about reptiles; field guides to many species around San Diego; list of books for teachers and kids.

Conservation

Books

Asimov, Isaac. *Why Are Animals Endangered?* Milwaukee, WI: Gareth Stevens, Inc., 1993.

———. *Why Are the Rain Forests Vanishing?* Milwaukee, WI: Gareth Stevens, Inc., 1992.

Bloyd, Sunni. *Endangered Species.* San Diego, CA: Lucent Books, 1989.

Challand, Helen J. *Disappearing Wetlands.* Chicago, IL: Children's Press, 1992.

———. *Vanishing Forests.* Chicago, IL: Children's Press, 1991.

Chandler, Gary, and Kevin Graham. *Guardians of Wildlife.* New York, NY: Twenty-First Century Books, 1996.

Duffy, Trent. *The Vanishing Wetlands.* New York, NY: Franklin Watts, 1994.

Gallant, Roy A. *Earth's Vanishing Forests.* New York, NY: Macmillan Publishing Company, 1991.

Hamilton, Garry. *Frog Rescue: Changing the Future for Endangered Wildlife.* Buffalo, NY: Firefly Books, 2004.

Haywood, Karen. *Crocodiles and Alligators (Endangered).* Tarrytown, NY: Benchmark Books, 2010.

Hodgkins, Fran. *Animals Among Us: Living with Suburban Wildlife.* North Haven, CT: Linnet Books, 2000.

Hoyt, Erich. *Extinction A-Z.* Hillside, NJ: Enslow Publishers, Inc., 1991.

Kalman, Bobbie. *Endangered Sea Turtles.* New York, NY: Crabtree Publishing Company, 2004.

Lasky, Kathryn. *Interrupted Journey: Saving Endangered Sea Turtles.* Cambridge, MA: Candlewick Press, 2001.

Levy, Charles. *Endangered Species — Crocodiles and Alligators.* Secaucus, NJ: Chartwell Books, 1991.

Mara, William P. *The Fragile Frog.* Morton Grove, IL: Albert Whitman & Company, 1996.

Mutel, Cornelia F., and M. M. Rodgers. *Our Endangered Planet: Tropical Rain Forests.* Minneapolis, MN: Lerner Publications Company, 1991.

Patent, Dorothy H. *Biodiversity.* New York, NY: Clarion Books, 1996.

Petersen, Christine. *Conservation.* New York, NY: Scholastic, Inc., 2004.

Phillips, Kathryn. *Tracking the Vanishing Frogs.* New York, NY: St. Martin's Press, Inc, 1994.

Phillips, Pamela. *The Great Ridley Rescue.* Missoula, MT: Mountain Press, 1988.

Pringle, Laurence. *Saving Our Wildlife.* Hillside, NJ: Enslow Publishers, Inc., 1990.

Pringle, Laurence O. *Living Treasure: Saving Earth's Threatened Biodiversity.* New York, NY: Morrow Junior Books, 1991.

Schueler, Donald G. *The Gopher Tortoise.* Berkeley Heights, NJ: Enslow Publishers, Inc., 2003.

Seibert, Patricia. *Toad Overload: A True Tale of Nature Knocked Off Balance in Australia.* Brookfield, CT: Millbrook, 1995.

Silver, Donald. *Why Save the Rain Forest?* New York, NY: Julian Messner, 1993.

Stefoff, Rebecca. *Extinction.* New York, NY: Chelsea House Publishers, 1992.

Tesar, Jenny. *Shrinking Forests.* New York, NY: Facts on File, 1991.

Thomas, Peggy. *Reptile Rescue.* Brookfield, CT: Twenty-First Century Books, 2000.

Wolkomir, Joyce R., and Richard Wolkomir. *Junkyard Bandicoots and Other Tales of the World's Endangered Species.* New York, NY: John Wiley & Sons, Inc., 1992.

Web Sites

www.eco-pros.com
Focus is on environmental education; information about the environment and how you can protect it.

www.fws.gov/kids/
U. S. Fish and Wildlife Service Kids Corner. Great site for students and teachers to learn about endangered species and how to help protect animals.

www.greenscreen.org
Urban Ecology Institute. Facts, activities, and stories about the environment for kids; resources for teachers; newsletter — nature news, by kids for kids.

www.kidsforsavingearth.org
Environmental education: conservation, endangered species, ecological concerns. Find out what you can do to help.

www.yptenc.org.uk
Young People's Trust for the Environment. Site designed to encourage young people's understanding of the environment; facts about animals and the environment; conservation.

Appendix II

Conservation Organizations

Conservation International
  2011 Crystal Drive, Suite 500
  Arlington, VA 22202
  Tel. 800-429-5660
  www.conservation.org

Defenders of Wildlife
  1130 17th St., NW
  Washington, DC 20036
  Tel. 202-682-9400
  www.defenders.org

Environmental Defense Fund
  257 Park Ave. S
  New York, NY 10010
  Tel. 212-505-2100
  www.environmentaldefense.org

Friends of the Earth
  1100 15th St., NW, 11th Floor
  Washington, DC 20005
  Tel. 202-783-7400
  www.foe.org

Greenpeace USA
  702 H. Street NW
  Washington, DC 20001
  Tel. 202-462-1177
  www.greenpeace.org

National Audubon Society
  225 Varick Street
  New York, NY 10014
  Tel. 212-979-3000
  www.audubon.org

National Resources Defense Council
  40 W. 20th St.
  New York, NY 10011
  Tel. 212-727-2700
  www.nrdc.org

National Wildlife Federation
  11100 Wildlife Center Drive
  Reston, VA 20190-5362
  Tel. 800-822-9919
  www.nwf.org

Nature Conservancy, The
  4245 North Fairfax Drive, Suite 100
  Arlington, VA 22203-1606
  Tel. 800-628-6860
  www.nature.org

Rainforest Action Network
  221 Pine St., Suite 500
  San Francisco, CA 94104
  Tel. 415-398-4404
  www.ran.org

Rainforest Alliance
665 Broadway, Suite 500
New York, NY 10012
Tel. 212-677-1900
www.rainforest-alliance.org

Save the Frogs
303 Potrero Street, #51
Santa Cruz, CA 95060
Tel. 831-621-6215
www.savethefrogs.com

Sierra Club
85 2nd Street, 2nd Floor
San Francisco, CA 94105-3441
Tel. 415-977-5500
www.sierraclub.org

The Wilderness Society
1615 M St., NW
Washington, DC 20036
Tel. 202-833-2300
www.wildernesssociety.org

Wildlife Conservation Society
2300 Southern Boulevard
Bronx, New York 10460
Tel. 718-220-5100
www.wcs.org

World Wildlife Fund
1250 24th St., NW
P.O. Box 97180
Washington, DC 20090-7180
Tel. 202-293-4800
www.wwf.org

Worldwatch
1776 Massachusetts Ave. NW
Washington, DC 20036-1904
Tel. 202-452-1999
www.worldwatch.org

Appendix III

Amphibian and Reptile Place Names

Alabama	Frog Eye, Toadvine
Alaska	Frog Mountains
Arizona	Frog Lake, Lizard, Rattlesnake Canyon, Snaketown
Arkansas	Frog Town, Toad Suck, Turtle Creek
California	Lizard Canyon, Toad Lake, Toadtown, Turtle Mountains
Colorado	Lizard Head Pass, Rattlesnake Buttes
Connecticut	Rattlesnake Mountain, Turtle Rock
Delaware	Turtle Pond
Florida	Alligator Alley, Rattlesnake Bluff, Turtle Creek Point
Georgia	Frog Call Creek, Turtle River
Hawaii	Turtle Bay
Idaho	Alligator Lake, Snake River
Illinois	Bullfrog Lake, Frog City, Rattlesnake Bluff
Indiana	Toad Hop
Iowa	Little Turtle Island, Lizard Lake
Kansas	Rattlesnake Creek, Toad Hollow
Kentucky	Snake Lick Creek, Viper
Louisiana	Alligator Bayou, Crocodile Bayou, Frogmore
Maine	Alligator Lake, Frog Pond

Maryland	Frogeye, Turtle Egg Island
Massachusetts	Great Snake Pond, Snake Hills
Michigan	Frog Lake, Toad Lake
Minnesota	Snake River, Toad Mountain, Toad River, Turtle River
Mississippi	Alligator, Alligator Town, Frogtown
Missouri	Anaconda, Cooter, Frogtown
Montana	Anaconda Range, Snake Butte
Nebraska	Snake River, Snake River Falls
Nevada	Alligator Ridge, Bullfrog, Lizard Hills, Snake Mountains
New Hampshire	Mud Turtle Pond, West Rattlesnake Mountain
New Jersey	Toad Creek
New Mexico	Alligator Tank, Rattlesnake, Snake Hills
New York	Lizard Pond, Toad Pond
North Carolina	Alligator River, Frog Level, Lizard Lick, Snake Mountain
North Dakota	Snake Hill, Turtle Lake, Turtle River
Ohio	Snake Hollow
Oklahoma	Frogville
Oregon	Frog Lake Buttes, Lizard Spring, Rattlesnake Creek
Pennsylvania	Frogtown, Turtlepoint
Rhode Island	Snake Den
South Carolina	Frogmore
South Dakota	Turtlefoot Lake
Tennessee	Big Frog Mountain, Frog Jump, Turtletown
Texas	Bullfrog Pond, Frognot
Utah	Bullfrog, Lizard Lake, Rattlesnake Butte
Vermont	Snake Mountain
Virginia	Frog Level, Frogtown
Washington	Bullfrog Mountain, Rattlesnake Ridge, Snake River Junction

West Virginia	Frog Hollow, Frogtown
Wisconsin	Alligator Creek, Frog Creek, Little Frog Lake, Turtle Lake
Wyoming	Alligator Rock, Frog Suck, Lizard Head Meadows, Rattlesnake Hills

These are just a few examples. Can you find more?

Appendix IV

Credits for Photographs

Brady Barr: Plate 13

Dick Bartlett: Figures 1 (both), 6, 13, 29, 31, 38, 41, 44, 47, 48, 49, 50, 53, 57, 58, 59, 63, 72, 74, 77, 78, 79, 82, 84, 90, 91, 95, 109, 110, 113, 114, 117, 118, 120, 121, 129, 134; Plates 1 (top left, middle left), 4 (bottom right), 5 (top), 6 (top right), 7 (top right, bottom), 8 (top left, top right), 10 (bottom), 14 (middle left, middle right, bottom), 15 (top, bottom), 16 (top left, bottom)

Judith Bryja and the Houston Zoo: Figure 7; Plate 8 (bottom)

Marty Crump: Figures 3, 5, 9, 10 (bottom), 11, 14 (top left), 17 (top, bottom), 19, 21, 23, 24 (top, bottom), 33 (left), 37, 39, 43 (top), 52, 66, 67, 68, 69, 70, 73, 75, 83, 85, 86, 87, 89, 98, 99, 103, 107, 112, 125, 126, 127, 131, 132; Plates 1 (top right, bottom), 4 (top right, bottom left), 5 (bottom), 6 (top left), 9 (bottom), 11 (top), 12 (top left, top right)

Danté Fenolio: Figures 4, 10 (top), 14 (bottom), 22, 26, 27, 28, 30, 42, 46, 54, 55 (top, bottom), 60, 64, 65, 71, 88, 101, 133; Plates 1 (middle right), 2 (top), 3 (top left, top right), 3 (middle left, middle right), 4 (top left), 6 (bottom), 7 (top left), 9 (top, middle left), 10 (top), 12 (bottom), 14 (top)

Karen Hackler: Figure 97

Bob Henderson: Figure 76

Joe Mitchell: Figures 2, 8, 12, 14 (top right), 16, 18, 20, 25, 32, 33 (right), 34, 35, 36, 40, 43 (bottom), 51, 56, 61, 92, 94, 96, 100, 106, 108, 111, 116, 123, 128, 130, 135; Plates 2 (bottom), 3 (bottom), 9 (middle right), 11 (bottom), 16 (top right)

Bekky Muscher: Figures 122, 124

Rich Sajdak: Figure 115

Front Cover: Upper top left: tree boa (Danté Fenolio); Lower top left: Rio Cauca caecilian (Danté Fenolio); Top middle: Amazon River frog (Marty Crump); Upper top right: green tree frog (Danté Fenolio); Lower top right: California tiger salamander (Danté Fenolio); Middle left: American alligator (Dick Bartlett); Middle right: Galápagos tortoise (Marty Crump); Bottom: green iguanas (Dick Bartlett)

Back Cover: Top: veiled chameleon (Dick Bartlett); Bottom: Komodo dragon (Judith Bryja and the Houston Zoo)

Glossary

Words defined in the glossary are italicized in the text for their first appearance in each chapter.

Acid rain — rain that is acidic due to pollutants, especially sulfuric acid and nitric acid

Adaptable — able to adjust to changes

Amnion — membrane that encloses a reptile embryo in fluid (bird and mammal embryos also have an amnion; fishes and amphibians do not)

Amplexus — frog mating position in which the male climbs onto the female's back and clasps her with his legs

Antivenin — substance that counteracts a snake's venom

Aquatic — living in the water

Arboreal — living in the trees

Camouflaged — blending in with the surroundings

Carapace — top part of a turtle's shell

Carnivorous — feeding on animal matter

Class — major division of a subphylum used in scientific classification; amphibians belong to the class Amphibia, and reptiles belong to the class Reptilia

Colonial nester — animal that joins others in a large group to lay its eggs

Complex life cycle — life cycle in which the animal passes through a larval stage before becoming an adult; the larval and adult stages differ in body form, and the stages often live in different environments

Conservation — protection and careful use of natural resources so that they will still be available far into the future

Conservation easement — agreement made between the government or a conservation organization and a landowner on how private land will be used; landowner often receives money or tax benefit in return for not developing the land

Deforestation — cutting and clearing away of forests

Dewlap — throat fan in lizards; males spread out the fan in display to females and other males

Direct development — all development takes place within the egg; instead of a larval stage, a miniature of the adult form hatches from the egg

Diurnal — active during the day

Ecosystem — all of the living organisms that live in a given geographic area and the non-living features (for example, climate and nutrients) that affect those organisms

Ecotourism — tourism based on natural history

Ectothermic — depending on external (outside) source of heat to warm the body; generally the source of heat is the sun

Endangered — in danger of extinction throughout all or most of a species' range

Endothermic — having built-in control of body temperature; producing heat chemically inside the body to maintain a constant, high body temperature

Evolution — change in the genetic make-up of a population over time

Farming operation — initial supply of animals is collected from the wild and bred in captivity; some of the captive-bred young are saved for future breeding, the rest are sold; does not require a continuing supply of animals taken from the wild

Food chain — single pathway of energy from one organism to another in an ecosystem

Food web — complex pathways of energy among many species in an ecosystem; made up of many interconnected food chains

Fossorial — burrowing under the ground

Head-starting — program of hatching eggs in captivity and then raising the young until they are large enough to be less vulnerable to predators; at that point the juveniles are released into the wild

Herbivorous — feeding on plant matter

Herpetologist — scientist who studies amphibians and reptiles

Herpetology — scientific study of amphibians and reptiles

Home range — area within which an animal moves about in its daily activities to find food and shelter

Invertebrate — informal term used for an animal other than a vertebrate; invertebrates do not have backbones composed of vertebrae (for example, a worm, an insect, a crayfish, or a spider)

Jacobson's organ — sense organ in the roof of lizards' and snakes' mouths; detects chemicals

Keratin — hard protein substance found in the scales of reptiles and scutes of turtles (and in birds' feathers and humans' fingernails)

Life cycle — series of stages that an animal passes through in its lifetime

Metamorphosis — process of transforming, or changing, from the larval body form to the adult body form

Nocturnal — active at night

Omnivorous — feeding on both plant and animal matter

Order — major subdivision of a class used in scientific classification; Amphibia is divided into three orders, and Reptilia is divided into four orders

Oviparous — egg-laying

Ozone — form of oxygen; the ozone layer of Earth's atmosphere blocks most of the ultraviolet (UV) radiation from striking Earth's surface

Parasitism — long-term relationship between two organisms in which one (the parasite) benefits and the other (the host) is harmed; the one that benefits is said to be parasitic

Parotoid — gland located behind the eye on a toad; contains a toxic secretion

Permeable skin — substances can enter and pass back out easily

Plastron — lower part of a turtle's shell

Poisonous — having toxin in the skin

Population — individuals of a species that live together and thus could potentially mate with one another

Population density — number of individuals in a population

Ranching operation — eggs or hatchlings are taken from the wild and raised in captivity to be sold later; because adults are not bred in captivity, the operation requires a continuing supply of wild animals

Regenerate — grow back

Scutes — plates made from keratin that cover a turtle's shell

Specialized — able to survive only within a narrow set of conditions

Species — all the individuals that could breed successfully with one another if they were all in the same place but are not able to breed with members of other species

Sustainable harvesting — removing (hunting or collecting) animals from a population in such a way that the population will still be there long into the future

Tail autotomy — ability to lose part of the tail voluntarily (many salamanders and lizards drop part of their tails as a defense against predators)

Terrestrial — living on land

Threatened — likely to become endangered within the near future

Venomous — having toxin in glands in the mouth; toxin is chewed or injected into prey or predator through teeth or fangs

Vertebrate — member of the subphylum Vertebrata; most vertebrates have backbones made up of vertebrae (for example, fishes, amphibians, reptiles, birds, and mammals)

Viviparous — giving birth to live young (as opposed to laying eggs)

Vocal sac — pouch in the throat area of a male frog that fills with air when he calls

Main Sources Consulted

– in addition to more than 100 scientific papers

Beebee. T. J. C. *Ecology and Conservation of Amphibians*. London, UK: Chapman & Hall, 1996.

Collins, James P., and Martha L. Crump. *Extinction in Our Times: Global Amphibian Decline*. New York, NY: Oxford University Press, 2009.

Cooksey, G. *Endangered Species: Must They Disappear?* Information Plus Reference Series. Farmington Hills, MI: Gale Group, 2001.

Duellman, William E., and Linda Trueb. *Biology of Amphibians*. New York, NY: McGraw-Hill Book Company, 1986.

Greene, Harry W. *Snakes: The Evolution of Mystery in Nature*. Berkeley, CA: University of California Press, 1997.

Hutchins, M., W. E. Duellman, and N. Schlager (eds.). *Grzimek's Animal Life Encyclopedia*, 2nd edition. Volume 6, Amphibians. Farmington Hills, MI: Gale Group, 2003.

Mattison, Chris. *Lizards of the World*. New York, NY: Facts on File, 1989.

Miller, G. Tyler, Jr. *Living in the Environment*. Pacific Grove, CA: Brooks/Cole Publishing Company, 2000.

National Research Council. *Decline of the Sea Turtles: Causes and Prevention*. Washington, DC: National Academy Press, 1990.

Pough, F. Harvey, Robin M. Andrews, John E. Cadle, Martha L. Crump, Alan H. Savitzky, and Kentwood D. Wells. *Herpetology*. Upper Saddle River, NJ: Prentice Hall, 2004.

Pough, F. Harvey, John B. Heiser, and William N. McFarland. *Vertebrate Life*. Upper Saddle River, NJ: Prentice Hall, 1996.

Reading, R. P., and B. Miller (eds.). *Endangered Animals: A Reference Guide to Conflicting Issues*. Westport, CT: Greenwood Press, 2000.

Stebbins, Robert C., and Nathan W. Cohen. *A Natural History of Amphibians*. Princeton, NJ: Princeton University Press, 1995.

World Resources 2000–2001: People and Ecosystems: The Fraying Web of Life. New York, NY: Elsevier Science, 2000.

Zug, G. R., L. J. Vitt, and J. P. Caldwell. *Herpetology: An Introductory Biology of Amphibians and Reptiles*. New York, NY: Academic Press, 2001.

Index

— Pages with photographs and illustrations in the text, and color plates, appear in boldface type.